MARK CHRISTOPHER CHANDLER

THE ABILITY TO KILL

Also by Eric Ambler

Novels

The Dark Frontier
Uncommon Danger
Epitaph for a Spy
Cause for Alarm
The Mask of Dimitrios
Journey into Fear
Judgement on Deltchev
The Schirmer Inheritance
The Night-Comers
Passage of Arms
The Light of Day
The Ability to Kill (Essays)
A Kind of Anger
To Catch a Spy (Ed.)
Dirty Story
The Intercom Conspiracy
The Levanter
Doctor Frigo
Send No More Roses
The Care of Time

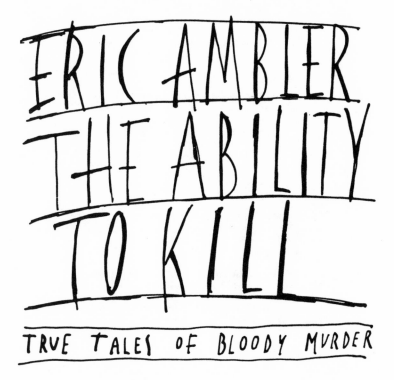

ERIC AMBLER
THE ABILITY TO KILL

TRUE TALES OF BLOODY MURDER

THE MYSTERIOUS PRESS

New York • London

The Mysterious Press, 129 West 56th Street, New York, N.Y. 10019

This Mysterious Press edition is published by arrangement with
The Bodley Head Ltd., 10 Earlham Street, London WC2

Printed in the United States of America

First Printing: October 1987

10 9 8 7 6 5 4 3 2 1

Library of Congress Cataloging-in-Publication Data

Ambler, Eric, 1909-
    The ability to kill.

    Contents: The ability to kill — The reporter —
Dr. Finch and Miss Tregoff — [etc.]
    I. Title.
PR6001.M48A65   1987   823'.912   87-42698
ISBN 0-89296-238-0

To

NELLIE WILLIAMS

with much affection

ACKNOWLEDGMENTS

It was Ted Patrick and Harry Sions, editors of the American magazine *Holiday*, who suggested that I write *The Lizzie Borden Memorial Lectures*. Two other pieces in this book were also written for that magazine. Parts of my account of the Finch-Tregoff murder trial originally appeared in *Life*. *The Magic Box of Willie Green* was first published in *Harpers Bazaar*. *The Novelist and the Film-Makers* was originally a lecture, an edited version of which was later published in *The British Film Academy Journal*.

The lyric from *The Merry Widow* by Franz Lehar quoted on page 187 is reproduced by permission of Chappell and Co Ltd (Copyright 1907 renewed), and that on page 198 by permission of the Robbins Music Corporation (Copyright 1934).

E.A.

CONTENTS

FIRST STEPS IN FACT CRIME

Although it is now generally agreed that the modern mystery novel had its origins in the works of Edgar Allan Poe, Wilkie Collins and Arthur Conan Doyle, it is not always realised that most early crime writing was what would now be categorised by the awards committee of Mystery Writers of America as 'fact crime'.

Mass literacy in the English-speaking world of the 19th century was the flowering of a quasi-religious movement, that 'Puritan impulse to teach poor children to read God's word for themselves' which came with the visions of a New Jerusalem. Those who were against such teaching, the illiberal old orders, said that poor children so corrupted would not stop at the Bible, that soon their grubby fingers would be reaching out for other books. The old orders were right. Once the new readers had, through the printed page, gained access to the world of ideas, there was no holding them. When they tired of reading religious tracts that only told them how sinful they were it was natural that they should turn for self-improvement to reading all they could about crime and punishment.

The format used by the early crime publishers was that of the tract, a thin, thread-bound, paper-covered booklet of twenty-four or thirty-six pages set in very small type. The selling prices would be in pennies. They offered verbatim reports of sensational criminal trials. Their authors, usually anonymous though often described as 'eminent', seem mostly to have been needy lawyers, or their clerks, aided by Grub Street hacks. In the early days they pretended not to take sides in the cases they were reporting. Of course, they did take sides, but they did so artfully; they were writing and editing for an emerging middle class that was both sanctimonious and prurient. It had a special liking for scandal in high places.

In London in 1836, for instance, a Mr Norton brought an action against Lord Melbourne—the great Lord Melbourne who was to become Queen Victoria's favorite prime minister—for having Criminal Conversation with Mrs Norton. Mr Norton claimed damages of £10,000. The 'full and accurate report of this remarkable trial by an Eminent Reporter' cost sixpence, and its 36 pages included a portrait engraving of the beautiful Mrs Norton, a granddaughter of the playwright Sheridan. Criminal Conversation was then a lawyers' term for adultery. In this case it was alleged that Lord M, who had used his influence as Home Secretary to get Mr Norton made a magistrate, regularly took advantages of that good man's absences in court to disport himself with Mrs Norton in her bedroom. The evidence of the Nortons' servants seems to have been all-important and mostly concerned with marks and stains on linen. The Eminent Reporter took refuge in prudish asterisks. A jury of City merchants stoutly refused to believe a word of it and conferred for only a few seconds before dismissing Norton's claim for damages. Their verdict was loudly cheered. Lord M was a popular figure.

By the middle of the century most notable trials were being reported in this way. The crime involved was often murder, but not always. The famous case of the Tichborne Claimant, for example, had its climax in a trial for perjury. It was, of course, a ready-made mystery of an old-fashioned kind, the tale of an unknown stranger from a far-off land turning up out of the blue to claim that he was the long-lost but rightful heir to a title and a fortune. All he had to do was prove his identity; and he went to extraordinary lengths to provide the proof. Public opinion was sharply divided for and against him. The case has inspired a number of novels. At the time it produced a flood of booklets and some remarkable early crime writing.

Some of the strangest was in a 24-page booklet entitled *The Tichborne Malformation*.

It must be remembered that in those days there were, apart from birthmarks, disfigurements and such things as tattoos, no visual aids to the making of positive physical identifications; no dental records with X-rays, no system of fingerprinting. All that the Claimant's supporters had going for them was a rather shaky legal declaration, made by the rather shaky dowager Lady Tichborne, that she recognised the Claimant as her son. Something more was needed. At one point the lawyers thought they had found it.

The malformation that was said to distinguish the Claimant and so clinch the proof of his Tichborne identity was something the doctors called 'a retractable penis'. The booklet starts off with a transcript of medical evidence given during the second trial, but given while the public had been cleared from the court. An expert witness, Dr Wilson, is being examined by counsel for the Claimant.

Now did you examine him yesterday with reference to the question of Malformation?

I did.

Has be a Malformation?

He has a Peculiar Formation?

What is that Peculiar Formation?

It seems like the end of an exchange of passwords. The witness suddenly becomes talkative.

The penis retracts in a most unusual degree, so that on one occasion when be passed water, which had been retained for some hours at my express wish, the penis was absolutely out of view, and nothing whatever of it could be seen but the orifice from whence the stream issued. Yesterday I found the member more turgid, but I endeavoured to push it back towards the neck of the bladder with which it is continuous, and I found it perfectly easy to push the whole member out of sight.

Have you anything further to add on the Malformation?

The witness had a great deal to add; he went into the anatomical details. For me, the images his evidence conjures up have the surreal quality of those early Max Ernst collages. The unknown crime writer who salvaged that transcript was ahead of his time. Nor did he confine himself to salvage work. His account of the attempts by the Claimant's lawyers to find witnesses who would say that the long-lost Tichborne had also had a retractable penis is masterly. The reader is left wishing that the Claimant with the Malformation had not in the end proved to be merely a fraud, an ingenious trickster with, poor fellow, not quite enough up his sleeve.

In America then the public taste for sensation was more austere and notable trial report booklets tended to concentrate as much on the nature of the punishments as on the revelation of the crimes. Accounts of hangings, especially those with speeches from the gallows or bungling by executioners, were given in great detail. Such booklets could run into many editions and competition between their publishers was keen. Barclay & Co. of Philadelphia were very aggressive in the field, and there was a crime publisher named Deary in Rochester NY who regularly advertised for subscription salesmen. For a while crime-writing almost became a branch of law-enforcement; trial report booklets were the new cautionary tales, the new tracts.

We can see the kind of changes that took place by consulting Thomas McDade's great bibliography *The Annals of Murder*. In 1833 the trial for murder of the Rev. Ephraim K. Avery of Rhode Island resulted in the publication of no less than twenty-one booklets and pamphlets about the case. The reason was that Avery had been acquitted and that his case had become a mystery. Yet, sixty years later, when Lizzie Borden was acquitted and her case had become a far more celebrated mystery, only four accounts of her case appeared. Edmund Pearson's famous essay did not appear until 1937.

There is no single, simple way of accounting for such developments. Of course, technical change had something to do with them. In the sixty years between the two cases the number, size and circulations of newspapers had increased amazingly, and many former publishers of booklets were now more profitably engaged in publishing popular periodicals that carried advertising. There were more crime reporters and more space for them to fill. This, too, was the century which saw the emergence of forensic medicine as a discipline and the birth of the great detective as an idea for a hero. The murder mystery as fiction, the solvable mystery, had become more appealing than the murder mystery of fact. There had been a parting of the ways. The mystery story was following a literary path; fact crime was off wandering in the byways of turn-of-the-century sociology. The parting, however, was temporary. The storytellers re-established contact with reality and the fact crimers took to the pleasures of making new sense of old evidence. There proved to be fashions in crime writing.

For me, the most interesting of all these changes has been in the public attitudes towards crime itself that has taken place during the last one hundred and fifty years. In the early 19th century the most hated and feared crimes were robbery with violence and (for those who lived by the sea) piracy. Domestic or 'brawl' murder (then, as now, the commonest kind) was, though deeply sinful, somehow less deplorable. The old fear of our being 'murdered in our beds' was a fear of robbers who might, through sheer fecklessness or stupidity, become killers. The crimes we most fear now are mostly those directed against all humanity. Our concern with individual murder has become a concern about the mind of the murderer.

In many states of the modern world murder is no longer a capital offence, and in every one of them at the time of the abolition of the death penalty it was predicted that its absence would increase the murder rate and render the crime no more interesting than petty theft. Neither prediction has been fulfilled. Murder rates still rise and fall along with other statistics recording the human condition. Trials for murder can still make headlines. Wilful, deliberate murder really is the most mysterious of all crimes, stranger than treason or genocide, much stranger than incest. That is why it is so much written and read about.

Some of the pieces in this book, particularly *The Lizzie Borden Memorial Lectures*, were written for *Holiday* magazine, and parts of my account of the Finch-Tregoff murder trial originally appeared in *Life*. *The Ability to Kill* I wrote for my own enlightenment and reassurance. I am one of those who think things through best by committing their thoughts to paper.

—*Eric Ambler*

The Ability to Kill

The Ability to Kill

Word goes round outside the court that the jury is returning.
Counsel, solicitors and reporters hurry to their places inside.
The prisoner is brought back into the dock. The jurors answer
to their names. The judge re-enters and takes his seat. The
clerk faces the jury.

'Members of the jury, are you agreed upon your verdict?'

'Yes,' answers the foreman.

'Do you find the prisoner guilty or not guilty of murder?'

'Guilty.'

Eyes go to the dock.

'You say he is guilty, and that is the verdict of you all?'

'Yes.'

The clerk turns to the prisoner.

'Prisoner at the bar, you have been arraigned upon a charge
of murder, and have placed yourself upon your country. That
country has now found you guilty. Have you anything to say
why judgment of death should not be pronounced upon you,
and why you should not die according to law?'

'I can only say that I am innocent.'

The judge places a square of black silk upon his wig and
addresses the prisoner.

'You have received a fair trial and have been found guilty,
to my mind rightly so, of the cruel and abominable crimes of
which you were accused. For those crimes the law appoints
one sentence only. It is that you be taken from hence to a place
of lawful execution, and you be there hanged by the neck until
you be dead, and that your body be afterwards buried within

the precincts of the prison in which you shall last have been confined. And may God have mercy on your soul.'

The court Chaplain intones an 'Amen.'

One of the wardens in the dock touches the arm of the convicted man. He turns and goes below.

For those who are not unduly disturbed by the prospect of a hanging, a useful ritual has been performed. Both crime and punishment have been internalised and the recesses of many uneasy minds have been purged, for a while, of some of their guilt secretions. 'But for the grace of God, there goes John Bradford.'

Goethe said that there was no crime of which he did not deem himself capable. Certainly, most men, and many women, believe themselves capable of murder. The belief is not wholly absurd. Given the necessary outlandish combination of persons and circumstances—a vile enemy, an ultimate infamy, the overwhelming moment of hatred, the self-righteous conviction that summary justice must be done, the deadly weapon to hand, and, possibly, the superego-solvent alcohol to loose the final inhibition—the thing can be done. It sometimes is.

Was that all that Bradford had in mind? I think not. When we say that we are capable of murder, we do not mean that we might just conceivably kill in a moment of ungovernable anger if someone put a loaded gun into our hands; we are admitting that we sometimes entertain murderous thoughts of another kind. The remains of that tin of arsenical weed-killer which we so carefully emptied down the drain—was it only fear of accidents that moved us to dispose of it, or was there another, less acceptable fear also present? Most probably there was. The belief that, simply because a person has murderous fantasies, he is automatically capable, given sufficient incentive, of committing a premeditated murder, is astonishingly widespread. In the course of allaying some of my own anxieties in the matter, I discovered that it is also quite erroneous. The will to destroy is common enough ('I wish he were dead.') and any reasonably good organiser can plan the deed; but the ability to put the plan into action, calculatedly to kill another human being, without the sanction of war or law, belongs only to a remarkable few—the sane murderers.

What is the word 'sane' worth in this context? According to the law, it seems to be worth a great deal. The McNaughten Rules—in essence, 'he knew what he was doing and he knew that it was wrong'—were able to find even the child-murderer Straffen sane after he had escaped from Broadmoor for a few hours and murdered yet another child. The Rules found Christie sane, and they found Neville Heath sane, too. In America, where in the past the English McNaughten Rules have generally been applied, some states are beginning to modify them. The Durham Rule of the District of Columbia, which, in effect, diminishes criminal responsibility where there is mental disease or defect, and the Vermont Statute, which recognises that a mentally diseased person may know that what he is doing is wrong but still be unable to stop himself doing it, are encouraging signs of change. Still, by and large, the law continues to distrust psychiatric explanations of behaviour. It prefers to believe in the concept of unmitigated wickedness that judges may denounce and the people punish with a will.

However, the murderers we are discussing here are certainly not insane, nor, unless we are prepared to stretch the phrase's application until it becomes meaningless, could they even be described as 'mentally ill.' If a medico-legal classification is needed for their characteristic and special ego-formations, 'moral defectives' has to suffice. They possess the ability to kill, for a financial or other material advantage, without passion and without remorse. They are the emotionally *un*disturbed. As G. J. Smith himself expressed it, they are 'a bit peculiar.'

In Smith's own particular case that was an understatement; but when he made it about himself, he was not admitting that he was a murderer, only allowing that his past relations with society might have been more satisfactory.

He was born in 1872, the son of a Bethnal Green insurance agent. At nine he was committed to a reformatory, probably for stealing. At nineteen he received his first prison sentence, for stealing bicycles. At twenty-four, after a period in the army, he was sentenced to a year's imprisonment for larceny and receiving. At twenty-six he married. He used his wife to steal for him by forging references and planting her in likely homes as a servant. At twenty-seven he took to bigamy. His practice, of course, was to 'marry' a woman, take her savings and disappear. Sometimes, he did not have to marry. On several occasions, having secured their money, he left the ladies high and dry after taking them on an excursion to some public place. There, he would excuse himself to go to the lavatory and then fail to return. When he was twenty-nine he was recognised in the street by his real wife. She had by then served a prison sentence on his account and had a score to settle. She had him arrested, and he went to prison for two years. That was his last prison sentence. Of course, he went back to stealing from women the moment he was released; but the experience with his first wife had taught him a lesson. He took care to move about more now—Brighton, Southampton, Bournemouth, Margate and other seaside towns—and he opened a second-hand furniture shop in Bristol to provide himself with a background and a base.

He was forty when he committed his first murder, that of Bessie Mundy. She had a trust fund of £2500 administered by an uncle. Smith found that he, her 'husband,' could only get his hands on the money if she died and left it to him. So what else could he do but kill her? There is nothing in his history to suggest that the murder was a psychological turning point for him. He seems rather to have been in the position of a man who had by accident hit upon a new way of solving an old problem. It is not surprising that, after seeing how well the bath trick worked, he should decide to use it again. No trust-fund difficulties figured in his subsequent murders. He married the women, insured their lives, made certain that their wills were in his favour, and then killed them. The extent of his emotional involvement in the deaths is best gauged by a remark he made after the first of them. Even as he pretended to labour under the shock of his bereavement, he could not help congratulating himself. 'Wasn't it a good job I got her to make a will?' he said. He also returned the bath he had used to the ironmonger's without paying for it.

In its artlessness, Smith's remark is reminiscent of the question J. G. Haigh asked the police when he realised that they were going to arrest him for murder: 'Tell me, frankly, what are the chances of anybody being released from Broadmoor?'

Smith and Haigh had, as well as moments of unwitting indiscretion, other things in common.

Haigh was born in 1909, at Stamford in Lincolnshire. His father was an electrical engineer. Both parents belonged to that religious sect which calls itself 'The Peculiar People'—the Plymouth Brethren—and discipline in the home was strict and sanctimonious. He was an only child. He disliked games, loved music and drawing, became a choir-boy and won a divinity prize. At the grammar school he was also known as a ready and resourceful liar with a taste for practical jokes of the kind which inflict pain on the victim. After he left school he worked for a time in a second-hand car showroom, then as an electrician in a cinema, then as a salesman. When he was twenty-five, he was arrested on charges of obtaining money under false pretences by means of a hire-purchase swindle. He was sentenced to fifteen months' imprisonment. When he came out of prison he worked briefly for a firm of cleaners before being sacked for dishonesty. He then went south and set up, under a false name, as a solicitor. He was quite a skilful forger and by selling non-existent shares managed to defraud his 'clients' of over thirty thousand pounds before he was arrested again. This time, he was sentenced to four years' penal servitude.

He was thirty-one when he came out of Dartmoor. It was 1940; but for a man of his ingenuity it was not difficult to secure exemption from National Service on the grounds that he was in a reserved occupation. He then took to stealing from evacuated houses. In 1941 he was caught and sentenced to twenty-one months' hard labour. As a convict on licence, he also had to serve the balance of his previous sentence. He spent his time in prison studying law and doing some curious experiments with mice; he found that they could be dissolved in sulphuric acid. He was released in the autumn of 1943, and went to work for an engineering firm in Crawley. The following year he started a sideline business of his own. He rented a basement in Kensington and fitted it up as a workshop for repairing the pin-tables and automatic machines used in some amusement arcades. They were owned by a man named McSwann. Of the six persons whom Haigh is known for certain to have murdered, McSwann was the first.

In his statements to the police and the psychiatrists who examined him, Haigh always insisted that it was only the desire to drink human blood which made him murder, and that the desire always became overwhelming following a recurring nightmare about a forest of trees dripping with blood. He also claimed, as if for good measure, that he frequently drank his own urine. However, if we omit those embellishments and consider only the verifiable facts, a more convincing picture emerges.

Haigh needed money badly. McSwann had plenty. When he told Haigh that he was 'dodging the call-up,' Haigh saw that the situation had possibilities. He ordered some carboys of sulphuric acid and a forty-gallon tank. When McSwann next came to the workshop, Haigh hit him on the head with a cosh, dissolved the body in the acid and poured the solution down the drain.

His next move was to go to McSwann's elderly parents, tell them that their son had gone north into hiding from the army authorities and that he, Haigh, had agreed to look after the amusement arcades in their owner's absence. The explanation was accepted. He now proceeded, using a forged power of attorney, to gain possession of all the dead man's property and assets. When the old McSwanns heard that he had sold some of the pin-tables and began to ask questions, he took them separately, and on the pretext of having arranged a meeting with their son, to the basement workshop, killed them and dissolved their bodies in acid. Having supplied himself with a further power of attorney, he then took possession of their property also. By murdering the McSwann family, he made more than ten thousand pounds.

His subsequent murders—of the two Hendersons and Mrs Durand-Deacon—followed the same pattern. All were done for profit. After his arrest, and when he had had time to realise that his vampire motivation needed support, he confessed to a further three murders. In those cases, he claimed, there had been no coincidental profit; the victims had been killed only for their blood. He did not know their names. The police could find no evidence at all that they had ever existed. The inevitable conclusion was that Haigh had invented them. The nightmare was described convincingly enough, and Haigh may very well have been troubled by such dreams; but the blood-drinking episodes that they were said to have engendered seemed to belong to a clinical picture sketched, too hastily, by Bram Stoker.

In Haigh's account of the murder of Mrs Durand-Deacon, he described how, after he had shot her, he collected a glass of her blood and drank it. He went on to describe his preparations for disposing of the body. Then, he corrected himself. Before pumping the acid into the tank, he had gone out to a nearby restaurant for a cup of tea. It was perhaps necessary to mention this. He was known in the restaurant and someone might have remembered seeing him there at that time. He wanted to appear completely truthful. But he destroyed his effect. Tea? On top of a nice glass of fresh blood? The defence plea of insanity never really had very much chance of succeeding.

William Bolitho wrote of 'the narrow chasm that separates the theft of property from the theft of life.' We sometimes speak of killing as taking life. A great many murderers, the insane as well as the sane, have been thieves before they became killers. Christie (another choir-boy, by the way) had a record of four convictions for stealing and obtaining money by false pretences before he killed; Neville Heath, H. D. Trevor, J. D. Merrett and Sidney Fox had similar records.

Is the ability to kill, then, only an extension of the ability to steal? In a sense, it would seem to be; but only in a very special sense. By no means all premeditated murders of the kind we are discussing are committed by persons with criminal histories. Before he became a murderer, Seddon was a hard-working insurance manager; Armstrong was a solicitor, Vaquier a skilled mechanic. Yet, between the mind of the murderer and the mind of the thief there is a discernible relationship. With all of us, death, money and aggression begin as elements of the same oral-anal fantasy system. Sometimes, however, the primitive, infantile valencies persist, more or less unmodified, as part of the adult ego-formation. Generally, given even a small measure of adjustment, the resultant conflicts constitute no more than a misfortune, in terms of neurosis, for the person concerned; but, in some cases, neurotic solutions will not answer, and some infantile components are accommodated without modification.

The danger inherent in such a personality structure is that of regression. Whether that process begins or not is decided by time and circumstances; but if it does begin it almost always continues. Murder is not the inevitable outcome; it may never be necessary; but it becomes, in the end, within the bounds of possibility. An American psychiatrist, Paul Schilder, has written: 'The child's idea of death is essentially deprivation. It is ready to believe that this deprivation, like any other, is reversible.' And of those who kill, he says: 'They are not more concerned about their own death than children are. It almost seems that these "normal murderers," who are not otherwise so badly adapted to their reality, show particular infantile trends in their reaction to life and death. One may say that they kill because they do not appreciate the deprivation they inflict upon others.'

Steal or be stolen from; kill or be killed.

To apply, as lawyers and prison governors so often do in their memoirs, the words 'callous' and 'cold-blooded' to men like Smith and Haigh and Seddon, is as absurd as to complain that a youth with an intelligence quotient of fifty is unable to grasp the principles of the calculus. Their kind of emotional incapacity cannot be related to any normal feeling situation.

Not many murderers make full and frank written confessions. Haigh's were certainly full, but they were made in order to lay the groundwork for a plea of insanity. Although they tell us a lot about what he did, or wanted us to believe he did, they tell us almost nothing of his thought processes. For anyone who wishes to catch a glimpse of what it is like to have the ability to kill, the confession of Alfred Arthur Rouse, written when he had resigned himself to death on the gallows* is more revealing.

He was born in London in 1894. His father kept a hosiery shop in Herne Hill; his mother was Irish. When he was six the parents' marriage broke up and thereafter he was raised by an aunt. There is evidence to suggest that the separation from his mother had a profound effect on his development. However, that did not become apparent until much later. He did well at the council school, and after he left to take a job as an office boy, he attended evening classes. When war broke out in 1914, he immediately enlisted in the army. The following March he was sent to France. Two months later, at Givenchy, he was wounded by a shell-burst in the head and leg. After a year in various hospitals, he was invalided out of the army with a disability pension which continued until 1920. At the periodical medical inspections which he underwent over that period, he complained of dizziness and loss of memory arising from the head wound, and insomnia due to the constant reliving of the horror of a bayonet charge in which he had been involved. He also had difficulty in flexing the leg. The latter disability persisted and the medical report of 1919 attributed it to neurosis, at that time an imprecise term the meaning of which depended on the doctor who employed it. It could have been used to convey a sour hint that ex-Private Rouse might be malingering in order to retain his pension. There was no suggestion then, nor later, that the head wound had caused any organic damage to the brain.

---

* It was published, on the day after his execution, by the London *Daily Sketch*.

In retrospect, and with some knowledge of his social behaviour from then on as a guide, it seems likely that the process of regression had already begun.

Before going to France he had married a St Albans girl. Nevertheless, during the few weeks he was overseas he managed to seduce a French girl of respectable family and make her pregnant. The child was born and he was later obliged to contribute to its upkeep. It was to be the first of many. Mrs Rouse proved to be an amazingly good-natured woman. No doubt her own inability to have children contributed to her tolerance of her husband's ceaseless efforts to get them by other women; but it was still remarkable. Of course, she could not have known all that went on; but she certainly knew more than enough. She must have loved him very much.

After his discharge from the army he went to work as a commercial traveller. He was a good-looking man and a persuasive talker. Soon, he was doing well and his earnings rose rapidly. Before long he was able to buy a car in which to cover his sales territory in the south of England. In the course of his work he would spend several days at a time away from his London home. He wasted not a moment of them. In her introduction to the Rouse volume in the 'Notable British Trials' series, Miss Helena Normanton said that the seductions of nearly eighty women were attributed to him. Most of them were chambermaids or shop assistants or waitresses—those who would be accessible to a smart chap with an officer-like toothbrush moustache (he claimed to have been a major) and a car. He used to tell them, smiling into their eyes, about his beautiful Irish mother. For the most part, however, these were not casual, one-evening relationships. There was nothing ordinary about Rouse's promiscuity.

In 1920 he seduced a fifteen-year-old servant girl, and a child was later born in a home for unmarried mothers. After a few weeks it died. Rouse tried again, and again the girl became pregnant; whereupon he insisted on marrying her (bigamously, of course, although she did not know that at the time) and setting up house in Islington. The second child, a son, lived. Rouse was a doting father. Unfortunately, he accumulated so many other paternal responsibilities over the years that eventually the boy's mother was obliged to sue for maintenance. That was in 1929. The long-suffering Mrs Rouse had a meeting with the mother and offered to take the boy to live with her. Rouse approved warmly and the offer was accepted. The bigamous marriage was forgotten.

No doubt Mrs Rouse believed that the new arrangement would have a stabilising effect on her husband. After all, this—*his* child in *their* home—was what he had always said he wanted. She did not realise that she was no longer dealing with a reclaimable man; nor did she know the extent of his difficulties. By this time, he had made at least two more bigamous marriages, and had, besides, so many illegitimate children scattered about the country that his income, substantial though it was, was insufficient even to meet the maintenance obligations he had incurred by court orders. He had never disputed paternity, and had always tried to do his best for both women and children. There were just too many of them.

The crisis came the following year.

In the spring, he seduced a young Welsh nurse, a probationer in a London hospital. This was a mistake. Hitherto, he had had no trouble dealing with outraged fathers or avenging brothers; it is not hard to elude the economically impotent. He now discovered, however, that this girl's father was a colliery owner of some importance. When she became pregnant, it seemed prudent to let her write to her father and tell him that she had also become Mrs Rouse. The pair then went to Wales so that Rouse could meet the family. The family

accepted philosophically what they thought to be the situation, and it was arranged that the daughter should stay with
them until the new house, which Rouse said he had just
bought for her, was ready for occupation. That would be early
in November.

It was then June. He returned to London a worried man.
He had managed to lie his way out of an awkward situation;
but he knew that the relief was only temporary. To add to his
troubles, another of his women, who had already borne him
one child, was expecting again. That would mean more maintenance to pay. And then there was the one in Southampton,
the one in Birmingham, the one in Leicester—the list was end-
less. If he did not keep the promises he had made in Wales and
the angry colliery owner started an investigation, anything
might happen.

He had been jolted, probably for the first time, into some
sort of recognition of his total predicament. As he began to
cast about for ways of getting out of it, the regressive process
accelerated.

That same month he read in a newspaper of an unsolved
murder case. It set him thinking—from now on we can use
some of his own words—'It showed that it was possible to beat
the police if you were careful enough.'

He goes on: 'Since I read about that case I kept thinking of
various plans. I tried to hit on something new. I did not want
to do murder just for the sake of it.'

Naturally not; but what murder had he in mind at that
point? He was, as he explained, 'in a tangle'; and, 'there were
other difficulties . . . I was fed up. I wanted to start afresh.'
Then, why did he not do as so many others have done; simply
run away from the whole mess; just go abroad and disappear?

His confession gives' no coherent answer, only the glassy
stare of a decision made. In order to be re-born he had to die;

or, rather, someone else had to die in his place. He had hit on something new. He would steal a life.

Early in November, he picked up an itinerant down-and-out in a public house near his home in Finchley.

'He was the sort of man no one would miss, and I thought he would suit the plan I had in mind. I worked out the whole thing in my mind and . . . realised that I should do it on November 5th, which was Bonfire Night, when a fire could not be noticed so much. . . . When I said that I intended to go to Leicester on the Wednesday night he said he would be glad of a lift up there. This was what I thought he would say.'

On the Wednesday night, the two met at the public house as planned. Rouse bought the man a beer, and a bottle of whisky for the journey. He himself drank only lemonade. They set out.

'During the journey the man drank the whisky neat from the bottle, and was getting quite fuzzled.'

By two in the morning they were on the outskirts of Northampton.

'I turned into the Hardingstone Lane because it was quiet and near a main road, where I could get a lift from a lorry afterwards. I pulled the car up. The man was half-dozing—the effect of the whisky. I looked at him and then gripped him by the throat with my right hand. I pressed his head against the back of the seat. He slid down, his hat falling off. I saw he had a bald patch on the crown of his head. He just gurgled. I pressed his throat hard. My grip is very strong . . . people have always said that I have a terrific grip. He did not resist. It was all very sudden. The man did not realise what was happening. I pushed his face back. After making a peculiar noise, the man was silent and I thought he was dead or unconscious.' Rouse then got out of the car, poured a can of petrol over the man, loosened a petrol pipe, took the top off the carburettor and put a match to the whole thing. As the flames roared up, he ran.

Two young men returning home from a dance saw him a moment or two later on the road. One of them asked him what the blaze was. 'It looks as if somebody has got a bonfire up there,' was the reply.

But the unexpected encounter had disconcerted him. After it, he seemed to lose his head. Instead of going into hiding for a time, and then 'starting afresh' as he had planned, he went to visit the colliery owner's daughter in Wales. To her, of course, he was known by his real name. When he saw it published in the newspapers in connection with the burning car case—the car registration plates had not burned—he left hastily for London and a hiding place. But it was too late. He was known to be alive. Within twenty-four hours he was trying to explain to the police that it had all been an accident. He did not convince them. Four months later he was hanged.

The identity of the dead man was never established. Rouse, so fond of his many children, was not even mildly interested in the person he had murdered. His confession ends with a paragraph which reads like an afterthought prompted by a question.

'I am not able to give any more help regarding the man who was burnt in the car. I never asked him his name. There was no reason why I should do so.'

There is a petulant note to it. It recalls G. J. Smith's surly observation on being reproached for a similar want of feeling: 'When they're dead, they're done with.'

Trials for Murder

1

The Reporter

A Wimpole Street doctor tells me that a strikingly high proportion of his Rolls-Royce-owning patients are privately convinced that if ever they were to lose all their money and be compelled to work with their hands, they could immediately become perfect butlers. He calls it the 'Crichton' fantasy.

Most of us, of course, enjoy Mitty-like moments in which we see ourselves triumphantly employing skills—conducting symphony orchestras, cooking cheese soufflés—which we do not in fact possess. Usually, as with the Rolls-Royce owner, the skill in question is safely divorced from the dreamer's true abilities. There may be, and probably is, an underlying psychological relationship between the two; but it is unlikely that the dream of glory is ever going to be challenged by the reality of a practical test.

In the case of some writers, however, that danger does exist. Most susceptible are those with no experience of newspaper work. They are prone to special fantasies. Of these, the 'W. H. Russell,' which takes the dreamer off as a war correspondent, is currently dangerous only if the dreamer speaks an African or South East Asian language. The 'Rebecca West,' however, is a different matter.

It seems harmless. The dreamer is reporting a murder trial. There he sits in the press seats of a crowded court, gathering the facts, weighing the evidence, shrewdly anticipating counsel's next move, and watching that small muscle twitch in the neck of the accused. His novelist's (or playwright's) insights probe sensitively for the hidden truth, the reality beyond what is being said. His professional compassion, even as the murderer describes the trouble he had forcing the dismembered body of the child into the kitchen mincer, is there ready to invest the creature with human dignity. Beautifully balanced sentences appear, as if by magic, in his notebook.

Good, simple fun; until one day a terrible thing happens. A harassed editor takes leave of his senses, and the dreamer is actually asked to report a trial.

The day came for me eventually. The alleged crime had been committed in extraordinary circumstances, and the case had already attracted wide attention. An American news agency, serving the Hearst papers among others, asked me to report the Old Bailey trial.

Eagerly I accepted. Within twenty-four hours panic had set in.

The American in charge of the news agency's London office was a sleepy-eyed professional with long experience of 'wire service' operation. Over luncheon he explained to me what the assignment would entail.

I need not worry about the literal reporting of the case. He had already arranged with a British agency to share the cost (staggeringly high it seemed) of a complete daily transcript of the proceedings. This would be roughly edited, and teletyped to the New York office as it was received. My task would be to dramatise the daily progress of the trial, to report trends, highlight personalities, make the whole thing 'come alive' for Americans from San Diego to Portland, Maine. New York, he told me a trifle wistfully, had said that I was to be given a 'hunting licence' on adjectives and adverbs.

At the time, I did not understand what he meant by this.

Now, I think, I do. There is a tradition in American news-paper reporting which forbids the reporter to 'editorialise.' He may write only the received facts. This is not to say, how-ever, that he only reports the truth. He may, indeed must, report what someone has said, even if he knows it to be a lie; but he may not say that he knows that it is a lie; that is editorialising. The 'fact' which he is reporting is the fact that the statement was made. The theory behind all this is that it is not the reporter's business to tell the reader which facts are really facts, but only to report what has been said and done. It is up to the free and independent reader to decide for himself what he believes. The reporter who writes the 'truth as he sees it' is hell-bent for corruption.

The principle is admirable; its practice has drawbacks. One of the reasons why the late Senator McCarthy was able so rapidly and so easily to lie his way to power was that every-thing he said was always faithfully reported. The New York *Times* once acknowledged the problem, but also shrugged it off: 'It is difficult, if not impossible, to ignore charges by Senator McCarthy just because they are usually proved false. The remedy lies with the reader.' As Richard Rovere has pointed out, 'to many people, this was rather like saying that if a restaurant serves poisoned food, it is up to the diner to refuse it.'

What was meant by a 'hunting licence' then, was a pundit's right to comment on what was said and done during the trial; moreover I was given that right in respect of the one event for which it must always be denied by British editors—a legal pro-cess which is still *sub judice*. I did have sense enough to ques-tion that aspect of the job, but was assured that, as none of the subscribing newspapers had British editions, there could be no contempt of court involved. It was the only piece of re-assurance I received.

'We'd like a couple of pre-trial pieces,' I was told; 'say a couple of thousand words apiece. The first one should outline the case as it comes from the magistrates' court. The second should be a run-down on the trial personalities involved; the judge, counsel pro and con, Scotland Yard brass, the local police, the accused man, probable trial tactics and so on. Of course, when the trial starts you'll have plenty to work with. You'll have to keep the pieces fairly short though. Not more than a thousand words a day. And there's just one more thing I'd better fill you in on—the time factor. New York is five hours behind London so we should make the afternoon editions of the evenings pretty easily. Court usually recesses around four. As long as we start sending your copy through around four-thirty, we'll be in good shape. Timewise it's only New York we have to worry about. Farther west there'll be no problem. Of course we'll have a private line run in from the Old Bailey press room to the office, and you could dictate your stuff over the phone, but I think it'll be easier if you just walk across to the office when the court recesses. It's only a couple of minutes. We'll have a desk and a typewriter ready for you.'

I nodded stupidly. I am a slow worker. The composition of five hundred words in a seven-hour day is, for me, a fair rate of progress. Moreover, I write in longhand. I have never learned to use a typewriter.

On the way to his office I tried to explain these things, and said that I would not mind a bit if they decided to employ another writer.

That, he said, was out of the question. I had made a deal. Besides, New York was already selling the coverage in advance for syndication abroad. It was going great. Naturally, I was nervous. He was always nervous, too, before a big story. It was really very simple. All you had to do every day was to find a lead. The piece would then write itself.

My protestations of incompetence seemed to disturb him less than my inability to use a typewriter. How could a writer *not* type?

We arrived at his offices. They were on one of the upper floors of an old building in Fleet Street and consisted of one large room, almost entirely filled with teletype machines, and two or three glass-partitioned hutches. The noise of the machines was overwhelming. I was introduced to several men whose names I could not hear for the din. Then, I was given a stack of files containing all the available information about the case, and sent home to start work on the preliminary pieces.

Most fictional stories are constructed so that the climax is reached at or near the end. Newspaper stories, I now had to learn, must be written with the climax first. This, it is reasoned, puts the most interesting part of the story on the front page where it will sell papers. I was warned that it was no use my doing it any other way; sub-editors short of space would automatically cut from the end of the copy. To paraphrase an old precept; every news story should have an end, a beginning, and an expendable middle.

In practice, it means that you try to buttonhole the reader with some odd-sounding tit-bit of news—'In the Smith trial today the prisoner threw an egg at the judge,' perhaps—and then delay the explanation—that the egg was really thrown at a board held by an usher standing by the judge, to demonstrate a point in the evidence—until you have unburdened yourself of the other dull parts of the story. The bit about the egg-throwing is your 'lead.'

The week before the trial with which I was to be concerned began, I obtained permission to sit in the press section of Court Number One while another murder trial was in progress, and made some experiments in reporting.

2—A.T.K.

The results were not discouraging, and my anxiety about the speed with which I would have to work was to some extent allayed. I had discovered something which should have been obvious; selecting and presenting material was not as laborious a process when the material did not have to be invented first. There is a quiet snack-bar in the basement of the Old Bailey. I decided that I would go down there and try to get the main body of the daily piece written during the luncheon breaks.

It had been expected that this trial would be a long one, perhaps as long as two weeks. In the event, it was one of the longest murder trials in the Old Bailey's history; it lasted over three weeks. By the end of the first week it had become fairly obvious that the prisoner was quite innocent of the murders of which he had been accused. It was thought that the defence plea that there was no case to answer might very well succeed. However, it was rejected and the trial dragged on. By the end of the second week, I knew the Old Bailey snack-bar from the Cambridge sausage to the sardines on toast, from the table that wobbled as I wrote to the chair with the cigarette burn on the leatherette seat. I had also learned, too well, that having to go on writing about a trial as if the outcome were still in doubt, when, in your own mind, no such doubt exists, is one of the most exhausting journalistic exercises there is; and also the most demoralising.

I came to hate the teletype machines. Soon after four in the afternoon, I would reach the office and begin to bellow the day's piece into the ear of a man who was one of the fastest and most accurate typists I have ever encountered. Another man hovered beside me. It was his job to get the pages to the teletype operators as they were finished. Unless I snatched them from the typist first, they would be gone before I could read them through. Once, while on page two, I decided to transfer a paragraph to page one and was told that it could not be done;

page one had already reached Chicago. After that, I held on
to the pages until messages began to come from the machines
saying that New York was becoming impatient.

At the conclusion of the trial, the judge's last act was to
thank the jury for their patience and to free them from any
future liability for jury service.

He did not, of course, see fit to thank the acquitted man for
his patience during the proceedings, nor to express any regret
for errors of judgment made by the Director of Public Prosecutions. Yet, the jury had only been inconvenienced. The suffer-
ings of the innocent man in the dock had included, aside from
the mental anguish of the entire ordeal, several months' imprisonment, exposure to newspaper publicity of the worst
kind (French newspapers had referred to him, before the
trial which proclaimed his innocence, as every kind of villain)
and the destruction of his career. Had the legal costs of his
defence not been borne by a professional association of which
he happened to be a member, he would have been ruined
financially as well.

Nobody supposes that a legal system which presumes innocence until guilt is proved can function without sometimes
causing the innocent to suffer arrest and trial; and nobody
supposes that prosecutors and policemen enjoy those occasions, which can make the lawyers look careless, the police
incompetent (or dishonest) and which may seem to have
wasted a court's valuable time. It is even understandable that
the officials concerned with an unsuccessful prosecution should
try to preserve their postures of infallibility by referring to the
acquitted person as 'lucky,' rather than as innocent. What
does seem monstrously unfair, however, is that the innocents
should so often be required to pay cash for their 'luck'.

In law an indictment for a criminal offence is, in some con-
texts, referred to as a 'libel.' It is just that. But there are libels

and libels. The private person who loses a libel action usually
has to pay his victim's legal costs as well as the assessed amount
of damages. The Crown does not have to pay either. The
Crown may libel with impunity and shrug off all the conse-
quences of its mistakes. The person tried and found not guilty
must be content with his bare acquittal, no matter what it may
have cost him. Unless he was already a poor man before the
trial (and so entitled to legal aid), he will almost certainly be a
poorer man after it.

True, he may be able to recoup his loss by selling an account
of his misfortunes to a newspaper; but, generally, innocence is
a less newsworthy subject than guilt. There may be more
financial hope for him if he resorts to another legal remedy,
that of libel suits (oddly enough) brought, not against the
Director of Public Prosecutions or the police, who are securely
privileged, but against the newspapers which over-reported his
case (with the eager assistance of the police and other pre-
judiced informants) before the trial began. It is possible that he
will have sufficient nuisance value to succeed in obtaining
settlements out of court. It is also possible that he will be so
sick and tired of the whole ghastly episode, and so anxious to
minimise the no-smoke-without-fire damage already done to
his reputation, that he will decide to accept his loss, avoid
further notoriety and efface himself as quickly as possible.

For the social and psychological damage that may be done
to the innocent man by due process of law there would appear
to be no practical remedy. Obviously, the Crown must be privileged. Certainly, improved methods of criminal investigation
and stricter police disciplines have tended to reduce the
number of persons mistakenly indicted. But, when the inevitable mistake is shown to have been made, it would seem that
the victim ought properly to be reimbursed for the costs of his
defence, if he has had to pay them. Whether he is, indeed,

lucky, or whether he has been most unlucky and much ill-used, the fact remains that a jury has found him to be not guilty. He is, at least, entitled to go financially unscathed.

I have since learned more about the cost of being tried for murder. This is not only a British problem.

In 1960, when I was in America, *Life* magazine asked me to write an article about a murder trial which had just began in Los Angeles. The defendants were Dr R. Bernard Finch and Miss Carole Tregoff. They were accused jointly of having murdered the doctor's wife.

The Finch-Tregoff trial (as it was called) was in the rich, rococo tradition of great American courtroom dramas. It had everything which that tradition demands: love, lust, passion, hate, greed, adultery, plots, counterplots, sensational disclosures. It had a cast of characters which included beautiful blondes, beautiful brunettes, Hollywood stars (or, at any rate, near-stars), hired killers, private eyes, and Perry-Mason-like attorneys. Los Angeles had given of its best; and intended to make the most of it.

I had been told that it was a pleasure to do a story for *Life*, and so it proved. It was assumed that you knew what you were doing and you were left to do it. If you asked for help you received it, promptly. One day I called for the police record of an obscure Minneapolis gangster, as well as for the details of the private financial arrangements existing between the defendant and his lawyer. Both sets of facts were delivered without fuss the same afternoon.

My only regret was that *Life* had decided to publish the piece before the trial ended. This meant that I had to be circumspect. Although I was allowed (as I certainly would not have been allowed in England) to use information not brought out in evidence at the trial, I could not say all the things I would have liked to say. It was not so much that the case was *sub judice*—the risk of being held in contempt of court was apparently slight—as the fear of attracting massive libel suits if the defendants were acquitted and advised that they had been given grounds. Obviously, *Life* was going to see that there were no such grounds. The number of 'if-we-are-to-believe's,' 'it-seems-that's,' and 'according to's,' that I was obliged to use, gave the piece, I thought, a shifty air. It is possible, now, to be more explicit.

The A6 murder trial interested me for a special reason.

Some years ago, I became involved, as a witness, in a case concerning the 'taking and driving away' of a car. The car was mine. A question arose as to my identification of the driver. The circumstances were these:

I was living in London at the time. One Saturday, two youths in their late 'teens knocked at the door and asked if I wanted my car washed. They regularly washed cars for several of my neighbours, they said. Their charges were reasonable. I told them that they could start the following week.

The following week they reported for work. I showed them the garage at the back of the house, and gave them the ignition key so that they could move the car out into the mews and use the hose on it.

An hour or so later, I went out to see how they were getting on. I found the car gone.

I did not call the police then. The young men had left their cleaning materials there. I did not know how long the car had been gone. They might just, at that moment, have driven out on to the road in order to turn the car before putting it back into the garage—an unnecessary manœuvre, but, providing they didn't do any damage, one that I didn't object to.

I walked to the main road. There was no car. I waited at the mews entrance for the best part of an hour before they returned. The car appeared to be undamaged. I was both relieved and annoyed. The driver said that he had gone to a shop to buy some polish. He could not produce the polish. When I asked if he had a driving licence, both of them scrambled out of the car and ran away. I still did not know how long they had had the car out, or where they had been. If the car had been involved in an accident, the insurance company would want to know who had been driving and if he had had my permission. I decided in the end that it would be sensible to telephone the police and tell them of the incident.

A detective-sergeant came and took particulars. I gave a fairly precise description of the driver and an indistinct one of his companion. Some weeks later, I was asked to attend an identity parade at the local police station. I had seen the pair on three separate occasions and in broad daylight, but my only clear memory was of the one who had spoken to me, and also driven the car. I had told the police this. The parade was held at night, under electric lights in a police garage.

As everyone who has ever been asked to make this kind of identification will know, it is an uncomfortable experience. Along with the wish to be helpful goes the determination not to make a mistake because of that wish. As you sit alone in the waiting room while the final preparations are made, you try to cast your mind back and clarify the relevant images in your mind's eye. After a few minutes of this, you become convinced that you are really so unobservant that any identification you make is bound to be incompetent. You consider advising the police to call the whole thing off.

A uniformed inspector was in charge of the parade, which seemed to be conducted according to a strict set of rules. There was a line of about twenty hatless young men standing on the far side of the garage and well away from the door by which I was brought in. At the door, the inspector asked me to go across the garage to the line, walk along it, and see if I recognised 'any of the persons standing there.' He was no more specific than that. He suggested also that I looked at every man in the line, and that I did not hurry. Then, he and the one or two other uniformed men who were there moved well away and stood where I would not be able to see them while the parade was on.

I walked over to the line and immediately recognised the driver standing somewhere near the centre. Nevertheless, I did as I had been asked, and walked slowly along the line from left to right. When I came to the driver, I took a long look at him to make quite sure. He stared through me as if he had never seen me before. I went on along the line. If the companion was there I did not recognise him. I walked back and stopped again in front of the driver.

I said: 'I recognise this young man.'

The inspector came forward and asked me: 'Where have you seen him before?'

'Driving my car.'

'Are you quite sure that this is the person?'

'Quite sure.'

Then the driver spoke: 'Mr Ambler has made a mistake.' It was said firmly and without indignation.

I recognised the voice, too. Of course, I did not know his name then. For convenience here, I will call him Frank.*

I repeated the identification. Frank insisted again that I was mistaken.

A week or so later, I attended another parade to see if I could identify Frank's companion. I failed to do so. On that occasion, I asked the police where they found the men to make up these parades. They told me that for a parade in that age group they were usually helped by volunteers from a local Territorial drill hall.

* Not his real name.

Meanwhile, Frank had been charged and the case was to be heard at the magistrate's court. Frank proved elusive, however. Twice the hearing was postponed because he had sent word that he was ill. About five weeks elapsed before I was called to give evidence. Then, to the magistrate's evident annoyance, Frank elected to be tried before a jury in a higher court. He was remanded on bail of fifty pounds. The money was put up by his father. They had the same lean, aquiline features; but there the resemblance ended. Frank was taller and had a flamboyant, challenging air. The father was wistful and gentle-looking, a craftsman of some kind who had worked hard and steadily all his life. On one occasion he nodded to me glumly when we encountered one another outside a courtroom.

After the first identification parade, I had suggested to the police that, as no harm had been done, and as the offence was pretty trivial anyway, Frank should simply be given a warning and told to behave himself in the future. The inspector's response had been cool and brief. At the jury trial, five months later, I learned why.

Frank had a record for taking other people's cars which went back some years. He had been caught and convicted a number of times. He had been placed on probation again and again. In fact, when he had taken my car he had still been on probation for an earlier offence. But the magistrate who had tried the previous case had also suspended Frank's licence and disqualified him from driving. By taking my car while that disqualification was in force, he had made himself liable to a prison sentence. It would be a very light sentence, of course; but the police hoped that it would at last bring him to his senses.

At the trial Frank's counsel cross-examined me at length about the first identity parade, and asked me if I recalled Frank's claim that I had been mistaken. I did, of course.

Frank's defence was a flat denial of the charge. They had the wrong man. The jury found him guilty and the judge sentenced him to seven days' imprisonment.

That evening the London newspapers carried reports of the trial with headlines describing it as a case of mistaken identity. One of them had a sub-heading—'Friend's Confession.' Both reports were accompanied by pictures, taken outside the court, of Frank and another young man, apparently of similar height, build and general appearance. The latter was the friend who had now confessed. Frank's counsel was to lodge an appeal.

The police, when I asked them about the reports, were reticent, relaxed and sympathetic. I had identified Frank, had I not? I had never been in any doubt, had I? Well then, all I had to do was to say so. The appeal would be in the Lord Chief Justice's court. They would let me know when. They were sorry that they had had to put me to such a lot of trouble —first, all those wasted days at the magistrate's court, then the hanging about at Quarter Sessions, and now this. No wonder people were reluctant to come forward and be witnesses.

I looked at the newspaper pictures again. It was easy enough to recognise Frank, of course. And why not? I had had all too many opportunities of seeing him since the identity parade. His was a now familiar face. Yet, the friend undoubtedly resembled him. There was the same long, narrow head, the same beaky nose, the same receding forehead. The personalities expressed by the two smiles were undoubtedly different; but, again, why not? The important question was this: if I had seen the friend in the first identity parade instead of Frank, or as well as Frank, what would I have done—might I have identified the friend as the person who had taken my car?

I did not *think* so, but, looking at the pictures, I was by no means certain. The fact that I had had three encounters with 'X' before the identity parade could mean little. I had been

interested in having my car washed regularly without the
trouble of taking it to a garage, but not all that interested in the
faces of those who would do the work. I had remembered 'X'
chiefly because he had been the spokesman, and because his
keen-eyed 'fast-sell' tactics had amused me.

The feeling that one may have been responsible for a wrong-
ful conviction is very unpleasant indeed. If Frank should
chance to read this, he may take comfort from the fact that I
did not enjoy much peace of mind during the weeks preceding
the appeal hearing. As it turned out, I had made no mistake.
Photographs, especially those reproduced in newspapers, can
be very misleading. Instructed by the court to look at Frank
and his friend side by side, I saw at once that the resemblance
was superficial. The bone structures of the heads were similar;
but height, build, complexion, colouring and posture were all
quite different. As far as I was aware, I had never set eyes on
the friend before.

Frank looked straight at me, keen-eyed to the last. I almost
expected him to say, 'Well, you can't blame a chap for trying.'
He seemed neither surprised nor put out when I confirmed the
identification. He had been remanded in custody for a week, so
his sentence had already been served. What he had hoped
to avoid, understandably, had been the inconvenience of a
prison record. It soon emerged that the friend, who had so
obligingly 'confessed,' had never before been in any trouble
with the police, and so would only have been placed on probation if he had been convicted. It had been an ingenious little
conspiracy. The court had harsh words for the pair of them.

What I took away was the memory of my uncertainty when
I had learned that the identification had been challenged. I
thought of all the murder cases I knew of in which far less
positive identifications had been used to build up cases for the
prosecution—men glimpsed at night and from a distance, in

artificial light and by persons with poor eyesight. And I remembered the relief I had experienced in court when I had seen Frank's friend and realised that I would not have to change my evidence and admit that I had been mistaken.

I went home and re-read Mr Sydney Silverman's account of the case of Walter Graham Rowland. It seemed a salutary thing to do.

Rowland was convicted at Manchester Assizes in 1946 of the murder of a prostitute named Olive Balchin. Her body had been found on a bombed site; death had been caused by hammer blows about the head. The hammer, a new one, had been near the corpse. Rowland had been seen by several witnesses in the dead woman's company shortly before the murder. He had had a criminal record. Above all, he had been positively identified by a shopkeeper as the man who had bought the hammer.

Rowland protested that it was a case of mistaken identity. The jury found him guilty. Asked if he had anything to say as to why the sentence of death should not be passed on him, he replied:

'Yes, I have, my Lord. I have never been a religious man, but as I have sat in this court during these last few hours the teachings of my boyhood have come back to me, and I say in all sincerity, and before you and this court, that when I stand in the Court of Courts before the Judge of Judges I shall be acquitted of this crime. Somewhere there is a person who knows that I stand here today an innocent man. The killing of this woman was a terrible crime, but there is a worse crime being committed now, my Lord, because somebody with the knowledge of this crime is seeing me sentenced today for a crime I did not commit. I have a firm belief that one day it will be proved in God's own time that I am totally innocent of this charge, and the day will come when this case will be quoted in the courts of this country to show what can happen to a man in a case of mistaken identity. I am going to face what lies before me with the fortitude and calm that only a clear conscience can give. That is all I have to say, my Lord.'

He was condemned to hang.

Four weeks later, a man named David John Ware, then in prison for theft, made a written confession that he had murdered Olive Balchin. He repeated the confession twice. The Court of Criminal Appeal refused to hear this evidence on the grounds that to do so would in effect be trying Ware without a jury. The Home Secretary ordered an inquiry into the confessions. Ware later withdrew them. Rowland was then hanged. He protested his innocence to the last.

Four years after that, in 1951, Ware went into a Bristol police station and reported that he had killed a woman. He added: 'I don't know what is the matter with me. I keep on having an urge to hit women on the head.'

This time he was believed. That woman, however, recovered, and he was tried for attempted murder. He was found guilty but insane, and committed to Broadmoor.

Of Rowland's case Mr Silverman wrote: 'What is certain is that no reasonable jury would convict him on the whole evidence as it stands today. On that evidence he is entitled to acquittal. That will not help him now. He is dead. That is the iniquity of the death penalty; its hopeless, ineluctable finality.'

2

Dr Finch and Miss Tregoff

West Covina is a residential suburb in the eastern section of the county of Los Angeles, California. Bisecting this wilderness of long streets, dusty palm trees, small houses, kidney-shaped swimming pools, dichondra lawns, and sprinkler systems, is the San Bernardino freeway. You may drive to the downtown business area of Los Angeles in thirty minutes. Economically, West Covina is plump; not portly, as is Brentwood, nor bloated, as is Beverly Hills; just respectably plump.

About a mile from the freeway is the South Hills Country Club. On the arid slopes beyond are houses belonging to some of the more prosperous members of the community. Until 1960, the home of Dr Raymond Bernard Finch on Lark Hill Drive was one of them. It is in the modern Californian 'ranch house' style and stands on the flattened top of a scrub-covered eminence with a commanding view over the Country Club car park. A steep, curving driveway leads down to the road. There is a heated swimming pool and a four-car garage. Early in 1959 Dr Finch is said to have refused an offer of $100,000 for the place. He would have done better to have accepted.

Shortly before midnight on Saturday, July 18 of that year, the West Covina police were called to the house. They found there a terrified and incoherent Swedish maid, and, at the foot of some narrow steps leading down from the side of the driveway, the dead body of Mrs Barbara Jean Finch, the doctor's wife. She was lying on the edge of a lawn belonging to the adjoining house where her husband's father lived. She had been shot in the back.

At 10.30 the following morning, and three hundred miles away in Las Vegas, Nevada, police officers entered an apartment a few blocks away from the Desert Inn Hotel and found Dr Finch asleep in bed. They wakened him, told him to dress and then placed him under arrest. At headquarters, they booked him on suspicion of murder, and waited for the West Covina police to come and get him.

Dr Finch, the son of a retired optometrist, was a graduate of the College of Medical Evangelists at Loma Linda, California, a surgeon, and part owner of the busy West Covina Medical Center.* I spoke with him during the trial. He was forty-two then, lean and tanned. The eyes were alert and intelligent; the close-cropped, greying hair made no attempt to conceal the bald patch on the crown of his head. He was a good tennis player and looked it. His manner was forthright. 'Call me Bernie,' he would say. The accompanying smile was muscular and confident.

He and Barbara Finch were married in 1951, both for the second time. She had formerly been his secretary and their extramural relationship had furnished evidence for both divorces. Both, too, had had children by their first marriages. Barbara's daughter, Patti, had gone with her when she had married the doctor.

Barbara Finch was eight years his junior and an attractive woman. She shared his enthusiasm for tennis and they were active and popular members of the Los Angeles Tennis Club. The birth of their son Raymond in 1953 might have been expected to cement their relationship satisfactorily. It did not. By 1957, he was complaining of her coldness, she of his

* A sort of private clinic run by doctors in partnership.

infidelities. That year they decided that, although they would continue to occupy the same house, they would, as far as their emotional lives were concerned, 'go their separate ways.'

Dr Finch's way took him promptly to a small furnished apartment in Monterey Park, another suburb five miles nearer town. He leased it, for $70 a month, in the name of George Evans. There was a 'Mrs Evans,' too; young and auburn-haired. They used to meet at the apartment every few days and spend two or three hours in one another's company. Sometimes it would be in the morning, sometimes the afternoon, depending on the doctor's professional commitments for the day.

Mrs Evans' real name was Mrs Carole Tregoff Pappa.

She was twenty then. A Pasadena girl, she had for a while been a photographic model. Model agency 'cheesecake' photographs taken at that time showed her posing in 'Baby Doll' nighties for a scent advertiser. She was startlingly pretty. At eighteen she had married James J. Pappa, a twenty-one-year-old cement mason and amateur 'body-building devotee.'* It had been he who had decided that she should give up modelling. Dutifully accepting his decision, she had taken a job as a receptionist. It had not lasted long. A month or so later she had gone to work at the West Covina Medical Center. She had become Dr Finch's secretary.

In 1958, Mr and Mrs George Evans leased a more expensive apartment for their meetings, and furnished it themselves. In January 1959, Carole Tregoff divorced James Pappa. In the same month, Mrs Finch went to a lawyer, and discussed the possibility of divorcing the doctor.

At that point in the story it looked as if events were proceeding in a commonplace way towards a commonplace conclu-

---

* He worked hard at his hobby. But for his lack-lustre smile he could have had a future in the 'you-can-have-a-body-like-mine' advertisements.

sion. Then, the character of the relationship between the doctor and his wife changed. The indifference, or passive dislike,
of the 'separate ways' understanding was suddenly replaced
by a bitter hostility.

There is little doubt of the reason for it. The community
property laws of the State of California call for an equitable
division, in case of divorce, of all assets acquired by either or
both partners during the marriage. However, when the divorce is granted for adultery, extreme cruelty, or desertion, the
court has discretion to grant the innocent party the lion's share
of the property. California judges have in general regarded it
as mandatory to do so.

Rightly or wrongly—presumably she was acting on her
lawyer's advice—Mrs Finch was taking advantage of this
situation to claim the *whole* of the community property, including all the doctor's assets in the West Covina Medical Center,
and the eight corporations which composed it, then estimated
to be worth $750,000. In addition she was asking for $18,000
legal expenses, plus alimony of $1640 a month, plus child
support of $250 a month.

If she succeeded in even 80% of her claim, and there was
little reason to suppose that she would not, the doctor would
be virtually penniless.

She *had* to be persuaded to accept a less punitive property
settlement agreement.

However, his arguments and appeals failed to impress her.
As the weeks went by, his attempts at persuasion became more
urgent.

In February, a nineteen-year-old Swedish exchange student,
Marie Ann Lindholm, had been employed as a maid in the Lark
Hill Drive home. One Sunday, Mrs Finch showed her a
blood-stained sheet and said that the doctor had tried to kill
her in bed. There was a bandage on her head. Apparently, the

doctor had relented, stitched up the wound and dressed it; but he had threatened to 'hire people in Las Vegas' to kill her if she reported the incident to the police.

After two days in bed recuperating, Mrs Finch moved out and took refuge in the apartment of a woman friend in the Hollywood Hills. She was, she told this friend, afraid of her husband. But not afraid enough, apparently, to change her mind about the community property claim. She went back to her lawyer, a Mr Forno, and on May 18 signed the divorce papers. Three days later, Mr Forno obtained a restraining order enjoining the doctor to refrain from molesting his wife, touching any of the community property or withdrawing bank funds beyond those needed for normal business and living expenses.

He was too late to secure all the bank funds. Two days previously the doctor had given the Medical Center business manager a cheque for $3000, drawn on his wife's account and apparently signed by her, and told him to cash it. The bank, after questioning the cheque, had paid over the money. However, in the light of what happened later, it is doubtful if an earlier restraining order would have been of much help. Dr Finch was in no mood to exercise restraint.

By now he was registered at a West Covina motel. Mrs Finch had moved back to Lark Hill Drive, so as to be with the two children. But he was a frequent visitor. During the weeks that followed, her friends at the tennis club and elsewhere heard tales of persecution.

To one of those friends, a television actor named Mark Stevens, she reported that the doctor would not only pick up pieces of 'bric-a-brac' and hit her with them, but that on one occasion he had 'sat on her chest' from nine o'clock in the evening until one in the morning—surely a record for this method of coercion. Mr Stevens, incensed at such ungentlemanly behaviour, offered her a revolver for her protection and a course of instruction in its use. Mrs Finch, saying that she was scared to death of guns, declined. Mr Stevens then got the jack handle from the back of her car and urged her to 'wallop' the doctor with that. She thought enough of this suggestion to keep the jack handle under her bed.

To another friend she confided that the doctor had threatened to push her over a cliff in a car which would then explode. When, in June, the doctor proposed through his lawyer a reconciliation to halt the divorce proceedings, she was sure that it was a trick. If he could get back into the house, it would be that much easier for him to kill her.

Nevertheless, an attempt at reconciliation was made and the two were interviewed together by a court marriage counsellor. The doctor claimed that he had given up his 'girl friend' and begged for another chance. Mrs Finch modified her position only slightly. The outcome was a further restraining order directing that 'all payments of income from the defendant's medical practice' were to be turned over to Mrs Finch 'to be expended solely' by her 'for the joint benefit, including payment of living expenses for both.'

This was not at all what the doctor wanted, and he never made any attempt to comply with the order. Moreover, Mrs Finch soon had her doubts of his sincerity confirmed. A few days after the reconciliation plea, he came to the house, hit her with a revolver and again threatened to kill her. The Swedish maid called the police. Dr Finch left before they arrived.

Mrs Finch reported the incident to her lawyer. At one point, she said, the doctor had tried to force her to get into his car. She added that if the doctor came to the house again, she intended to run for protection to her father-in-law's house, next door. On July 7 she signed a deposition to the effect that the doctor had failed to obey the order requiring him to turn over all his income to her. A subpoena was then issued instructing him to appear on a charge of contempt of court.

This document was not served upon him until a week later; but it is unlikely that the delay was of any consequence. In Las Vegas, there had already been set in motion a train of events which, at that stage, no ordinary legal process could conceivably have brought to a halt.

Miss Tregoff—she had resumed her maiden name—had left Los Angeles in May and gone to Las Vegas, where she was staying with old family friends. She had taken this step, she later explained, in order to 'get out of the triangle.'

She merely elongated it.

It was a trying time for the doctor. In addition to his exacting work as a surgeon at the Medical Center and the emotionally gruelling business of hurling bric-a-brac at his wife, he now had a lot of extra mileage to cover. With no good news for him to bring to them, even the Las Vegas meetings lacked the relieving gaiety he needed. As the weeks went by, and the tight-lipped reports and gloomy discussions of ways and means became repetitive, new elements of fantasy began to seep into his conferences with Miss Tregoff.

The family friends with whom she was staying had a twenty-one-year-old grandson named Donald Williams. A law student at the University of Nevada, he had been a childhood friend of hers. In June she asked him if he knew of any men in Las Vegas who were involved in crime.

He told her that a boy he went to college with had a friend from Minneapolis who was 'in the rackets.' Miss Tregoff said that she would like to meet him. Young Williams already knew of her relationship with Dr Finch, and that the doctor was being divorced. When she explained that she was interested in getting some man who would take Mrs Finch out and provide evidence to be used against her in the divorce action, he understood perfectly. One statement she made, however, did make him a trifle uneasy. Miss Tregoff said that she 'would be quite happy when Mrs Finch would be out of the picture permanently.' It made him 'develop an idea' that there might be violence involved in the plan. But he shrugged off his misgivings and agreed to arrange the meeting.

The go-between was a disagreeable delinquent named Richard Keachie. Later he was indicted in Las Vegas for violations of the Mann Act and the rooming-house ordinances* and for being a fugitive from justice. He disappears from the scene. Left in the foreground, with a polite leer on his face and a bottle of bourbon at his elbow, is the man from Minneapolis to whom he introduced her, John Patrick Cody.

He was born in Minneapolis in 1930. His police record, dating from 1946 when he was doing time in the State Reformatory at Red Wing, included nineteen arrests. They covered charges of drunkenness and disorderly conduct (5), suspicion of robbery (2), assault and battery (3), careless driving and other traffic offences of a more or less serious nature (9), and an A.W.O.L. charge from the Marine Corps. The record of convictions told a story of short-term sentences, fines and placings-on-probation. In 1958, however, his public nuisance value had increased, and he had been sentenced to a year in the Minneapolis Workhouse on a charge of passing a bad cheque. Three weeks later, he had escaped from the Workhouse and made his way south to Las Vegas.

What the record did not show was that Cody belonged to that rare and remarkable subdivision of the human species— the amoral realists with no illusions about their own frailties or anyone else's, and no sense of guilt. The odd thing about such men is that, having no pretensions to being less odious than they are, they sometimes achieve a kind of honesty.

* He was a pimp.

His own description of his normal mode of existence was that he lived by his wits. Specifically, he worked as a gamblers' shill, or decoy, when he had to, but preferred to pay his way by sponging off women. He was a heavy drinker with a pale, puffy complexion and empty eyes. His hair was sleek, however, and his clothes startlingly natty. He wore dark Italianate suits, and white satin neckties. He had his name embroidered on his shirt cuffs. A slack, lop-sided smirk completed the ensemble.

After the initial introduction, when young Williams and Keachie were present, Cody and Miss Tregoff had a number of meetings alone.

According to him, it was on July 1 that Miss Tregoff broached the subject of his killing Mrs Finch. His response was to quote a price of $2000 for the job. She countered with an offer of one thousand. He pointed out that he would need a hundred dollars to buy a weapon, another hundred for a car to get to the Finch house and at least two hundred more for travel and incidental expenses. After further haggling, they agreed on $1400—$350 down and the balance when he had done the job. Then, she drew maps for him showing how to get to the Finch house and the Hollywood apartment of Mrs Finch's woman friend. Asked how he would do the killing, he said that he would make it look as if it had been done during a robbery. A date was decided—the Fourth of July*—so that everyone else concerned could prepare an alibi. The next day, she gave him $330 and an air ticket, and he was ready to go.

At this point, it appears, his finer feelings got the better of him; or possibly he thought that, if he seemed to be temporising, there might be more than fourteen hundred dollars to be gleaned from the situation. He asked Miss Tregoff if she was sure that she wanted to go through with it. 'When I get on that

* A Bank Holiday week-end.

plane,' he reminded her sternly, 'you can't recall me.' But Miss Tregoff was unmoved. 'Good,' she replied, and wished him luck.

If Mrs Finch had indeed been murdered during the Fourth of July week-end, both Dr Finch and Miss Tregoff would have had excellent alibis. She had taken a job as a cocktail waitress in the Sands Hotel in Las Vegas and was working there. He was down in La Jolla, a hundred and twenty miles south of Los Angeles, ostentatiously forgetting his troubles by playing in a tennis tournament. He was in the doubles competition, with a clergyman as his partner.

Cody's Fourth of July week-end was earthier. Upon leaving Miss Tregoff, he cashed in the air ticket, drove down to Los Angeles and spent the holiday with a girl friend in Hollywood. He did not go near West Covina. All he killed was a bottle or two of bourbon.

On the Sunday, he returned to Las Vegas and reported to Miss Tregoff. 'She asked me if I had done the job. I said, "Yes" and she asked me how I had done it. I said: "With a shotgun." She then handed me an envelope with six or seven hundred dollar bills in it. She was smiling. She was very happy. It was the first time I had seen the girl happy.'

The happiness was short-lived. On Monday, the doctor talked to his wife on the telephone. She was very much alive. He called Las Vegas.

Confronted by Miss Tregoff, Cody professed incredulous amazement and insisted that he had done the killing. She was sceptical, but the doctor, who arrived shortly afterwards, was unexpectedly helpful. With remarkable faith in his hench-man's probity he concluded that Mrs Finch's woman friend must have been killed by mistake.

'He said a tragic error had been made,' Cody recalled. 'He told me to go back and do it right. He wanted to know how much it was going to cost to get me to go back and do it. I said I needed a weapon. He said he had a shotgun in his car that I could use, but I said no. I would get my own weapon. I agreed to go back and kill her. He told me to let her know what she was getting it for, to tell her, "This is for Bernie."'

Even Cody found this a little troubling. They were sitting on a hotel patio when this conversation took place. Dr Finch, who had been drinking something called an 'Orange Squeeze,' was quite sober. Cody, hitting the bourbon as usual, was just sober enough to make a maudlin appeal to the doctor's common sense.

'I said, "Doctor are you in love with Carole?" and he said, "Yes, very much." I said, "I can see the handwriting on the wall. Killing your wife for money alone (*sic*) isn't worth it. You ought to let her have every penny . . . you can take Carole to a new town and start up a new business, or up on a mountain-top and live off the wild. If the girl loves you, she's going to stick with you." But he said no, he wanted it done, that Mrs Finch had him in a bottleneck.'

There was also some rather sinister jocularity.

'The doctor told me about his clinic. He said after this is all over, if I was ever on the lam or hiding-out, he could put me in his clinic. I said, "That is sort of silly, after I have killed your wife, to put myself at your mercy. . . . I'd just as soon stay out of your clinic." And we laughed about it. But,' Cody added grimly, 'I meant it.'

After the doctor had gone, Cody downed another drink and gave Miss Tregoff some fatherly advice. '"You're twenty-two years old," I told her, "and you don't know what you're getting into. Murder is a pretty big beef."'

Brushing aside this understatement, Miss Tregoff replied that he might back out, but that 'if you don't do it the doctor will, and if he doesn't, *I* will.'

Some hours later Cody woke up on a plane going to Los Angeles. He had a hangover and eighty or ninety dollars more in his pocket than he thought he had had.

He spent another few idle days in Hollywood. Then, deciding that there was nothing to be gained from further encounters with Dr Finch—and possibly some front teeth to be lost—he left discreetly for Wisconsin.

It was a sensible decision. The doctor had by now leased an apartment in Las Vegas for Miss Tregoff—his 'fiancée' as he described her to the apartment house manager—and was driving up there more often. There were tactical as well as sentimental reasons for this. The doctor was at this time trying to evade service of the subpoena on the contempt charge. Until July 14 he was successful.

He was at the Medical Center when the document was served on him. It required him to appear in court nine days later on July 23. On Friday the 17th he left his car at a Los Angeles airport and flew up to Las Vegas.

On Saturday the 18th, he and Miss Tregoff drove down in her car from Las Vegas to West Covina. They went, according to subsequent statements of Miss Tregoff's, in order to confront Mrs Finch with the fact of their relationship (of which Mrs Finch had been all too obviously aware for over a year) and to try to talk her into an out-of-court property settlement agreement.

They reached Lark Hill Drive shortly after ten in the evening and parked the car at the Country Club.

According to Miss Tregoff, the doctor went up to the driveway of his house, and then called down to her to come up and bring a flashlight with her.

She did so; but instead of taking just the flashlight, she 'became confused' and took up an attaché case of the doctor's which she knew to contain a flashlight.

The attaché case was found near the garage the following day. It contained, in addition to a flashlight, two lengths of rope, an ampoule of seconal, a bottle of seconal tablets, two hypodermic syringes with needles, a pair of surgeon's gloves, a sheet of rubber bandage, a wide bandage, a wide elastic bandage, and a carving knife with a six-inch blade. All this was later to be described as a 'murder kit.'

When the doctor and Miss Tregoff reached the garage, they saw that Mrs Finch's car was not there, and concluded that she was out. In fact, she had gone to the tennis club early that afternoon and had dined out afterwards at a restaurant with friends.

They decided to wait for her. They did not go into the house. Miss Lindholm, the maid, and Patti, the doctor's twelve-year-old stepdaughter, were watching the Miss Universe Contest on television and remained unaware of them. Miss Tregoff and the doctor passed the time by playing with the dog, an elderly Samoyed named Frosty.

Mrs Finch returned shortly after eleven o'clock.

Miss Tregoff says that as Mrs Finch drove into the garage the doctor walked up and said that they wanted to talk to her. Mrs Finch replied that she did not want to do any talking.

Miss Tregoff said: 'She got out of the car and bent down. Her back was to me, but then I noticed she had a gun pointed towards me. Dr Finch reached behind his wife into the car, threw something at me which hit me in the stomach and yelled at me to get out of there. The object he threw was a leather case.'

Miss Tregoff says that, as she ran across the lawn, she tripped over a sprinkler head and heard Mrs Finch scream.

'I heard another sound from the garage and it sounded like Dr Finch was in trouble. I started back in quite cautiously. Then I saw Barbara on the right side of the car. She took off down the driveway. She had a gun in her hand. I ran back around the lawn. I was scared. I was afraid of being shot at. I guess I stayed there until about 5 a.m. while all kinds of police came around. I seemed to be paralysed.'

In the end, she left her hiding place, behind a large bougainvillaea, and made her way down the hill to the car park. Her car was still there. She drove back to Las Vegas.

Miss Lindholm's account of what happened is very different. She never saw Miss Tregoff and did not know that she was there.

Just after eleven the television was switched off and Patti went to bed. Miss Lindholm went to her room. She heard Mrs Finch's car drive in. A few seconds later, she heard Mrs Finch scream for help.

Miss Lindholm had some difficulty in expressing herself in English, and her accounts of the events of the next few minutes varied; but the general pattern was clear.

She ran out, thinking that Mrs Finch might have fallen into the swimming pool, or had some other accident. Patti ran out with her; but, when they heard the doctor's angry voice, Miss Lindholm sent the child back to the house and went on alone. When she reached the garage, she turned on the lights. She saw Mrs Finch lying on the floor. She was bleeding from a cut on the forehead. Dr Finch was standing over her.

As Miss Lindholm started towards Mrs Finch, the doctor grabbed the girl 'by the face and chin' and banged her head against the wall. A broken area of plaster on the wall seemed to bear out this part of her story. She was not clear what happened immediately after that. She was not sure whether or not she lost consciousness, nor whether she remained on her feet. She did remember clearly that the doctor ordered her into the car and that he had a gun in his hand. In one account, she said that he fired a shot to enforce his orders.

At all events, she climbed into the rear seat of Mrs Finch's convertible. At the same time, the doctor was ordering his wife to get into the front seat. As she got to her feet he told her to give him the car keys. Then he shouted at her: 'So help me, I will kill you if you don't do as I say.'

Apparently, Mrs Finch made as if to obey, then suddenly turned and ran out of the garage. A week or so earlier, it will be remembered, she had told her lawyer that if the doctor came to the house again, she would run for protection to the house of his parents. That was the direction in which she ran now. The doctor ran after her.

Miss Lindholm said he had a gun in his hand. Miss Tregoff said that it was Mrs Finch who had the gun.

There is no doubt, however, about the rest of Miss Lindholm's story. She got out of the car and ran to the house. Patti unlocked the door and let her in. At just about that time, they heard a distant shot. Miss Lindholm called the police.

Mrs Finch's body had only one shoe on. The other shoe, together with some pieces of earrings, was found by the police on the shoulder of the driveway above. In addition to having been shot in the back with a 0.38 bullet, Mrs Finch had two skull fractures and a number of bruises and abrasions which could have been the result of her being hit with a gun. A torn surgical glove was lying on the floor of the garage.

No gun was found. No one saw Miss Tregoff hiding in the bougainvillaea. Dr Finch had left.

At the time the police arrived at the house, the doctor was, in fact, on South Citrus Avenue, a few minutes' walk away, stealing a Ford car from a driveway. He abandoned it two miles away in La Puente, and then stole a Cadillac, in which he drove up to Las Vegas. It was about 6.30 a.m. when he reached Miss Tregoff's apartment. She had not yet returned. The manager let him in with a pass key.

Then, the doctor went to bed. He had had a tiring day.

Miss Tregoff says that it was on the way back to Las Vegas and over the car radio, that she learned of Mrs Finch's death. When she awakened the doctor and told him, he 'seemed quite shocked.' 'I asked him if he had killed his wife and he said no.'

Relieved to hear this, Miss Tregoff went off to work at the Sands Hotel, where she was a cocktail waitress on the morning shift. Some hours later, after the doctor's arrest, she was taken to Las Vegas police headquarters, questioned, and then held as a material witness. She made a number of statements. Eleven days later, after she had given evidence at the preliminary hearing of the case against Dr Finch in the municipal court, she was arrested on a charge of 'aiding and abetting' him in the murder of Mrs Finch.

An indiscreet conversation between two Las Vegas prostitutes led the police to question Keachie. In August, Cody was picked up by the police in Milwaukee.

The Los Angeles County Court building looks like the new head office of a prosperous building society. There are escalators inside as well as lifts. Courtroom No. 12 is spacious, well-lighted, and efficiently air-conditioned. There is no dock. Defendants sit beside their lawyers at a long table facing the judge's rostrum. Also at this table are the prosecution lawyers. The witness 'stand' is a throne-like chair placed beside the judge's desk and furnished with a microphone so that the whole court can hear plainly what is said. The jury sits to the left of the judge. The press box is on the right. A wooden barrier with swing gates separates all this from the main body of the court where the public sits. Over three hundred spectators can be accommodated.

American courtroom scenes in films and books had prepared me for most of the differences of lay-out and procedure. What

I had not been prepared for was the informality of Western justice.

Each defendant was in the charge of a uniformed sheriff (in Miss Tregoff's case, an attractive girl-sheriff) and they were brought into court via the public corridor. Once seated at their table to await the arrival of the judge, they were immediately surrounded by press photographers, television cameramen and reporters, who only moved out when the bailiff announced the judge's entrance. During the frequent and lengthy recesses, the photographers and reporters would move in again. Photography in court was forbidden only during the actual hearing; but during the recesses lawyers and witnesses could pose for pictures re-enacting the proceedings. As the trial progressed a circus atmosphere developed that even the regular crime reporters began to find disconcerting. One Los Angeles paper was running a series of 'impressions' written by Hollywood actresses—a different one each day.* The sight of those ladies, pad and pencil in hand, dark glasses removed and skirts hitched up becomingly, being photographed while they interviewed the eagerly co-operative defendants, made one wonder if this really could be a murder trial, if perhaps the whole thing had not been engineered by one of the studio publicity departments to promote a new picture.

The bearing of the defendants themselves did nothing to correct that impression. They appeared relaxed and unselfconscious, even a little bored. The smiles they exchanged now and again were fondly rueful. They behaved a little like a pair of newlyweds separated for the first time by different bridge tables.

---

* Miss Jayne Meadows was heard to say, after her interview with Dr Finch, that he was 'fascinating.' Miss Patricia Owens, after her interview, thought that Miss Tregoff 'was being very sensible about the whole thing.' That, at least, was good to know.

The Deputy District Attorney in charge of the prosecution made no noticeable contribution to the dignity of the proceedings. He was a lanky, soft-spoken, middle-aged man with the apologetic air of an amateur actor cast as Marc Antony in a charity performance of *Julius Caesar*, and worried about the draping of his toga. He smiled too often, as if to inform us that he appreciated the joke, too. He was, no doubt, a most capable lawyer. Unfortunately, he had a habit of mislaying his documents and exhibits. Photograph in hand he would advance on a witness. 'I show you this photograph of a Cadillac car,' he would begin sternly, 'and ask if you can identify. . . .' At that moment he would himself catch sight of the photograph, realise that it showed a house or a bullet wound, and break off. 'Excuse me, Your Honour,' he would say to the judge, and then pick his way unhurriedly through the contents of a big soap-flakes carton in which he kept his records of the case. If this failed him, he would cross to the courtroom filing cabinet, containing the already labelled exhibits, and try there. Usually, he found what he wanted in the end, but the delays were boring and gave the prosecution's case an indecisive air.

Mr Grant Cooper (for Dr Finch) and Mr Egan (for Miss Tregoff) were more impressive; Mr Cooper in particular.

His cross-examination of the Swedish maid was in the best tradition. The young woman was harassed and confused. It would have been easy for him to have confused her still further. Instead, he handled her quietly and gently, obviously earning the liking and respect of the jury as he did so. He threw just enough doubt on her recollection of events to make room for the defence's accidental death story which was to come later.

The stumbling block, however, was Mr Cody. If he were believed, the doctor and Miss Tregoff were conspirators with a very determined intent to murder. Accident would be out of the question. Cody's evidence had to be discredited.

With his record, it should have been easy. It was not. He could admit to the basest motives and behaviour without a trace of embarrassment. He was the defence lawyer's nightmare. It is hard to discredit the evidence of a man who insists so cheerfully on his own perfidy, his total *lack* of credit.

Cooper did his best. For example, he brought out the fact that the witness was an escapee from a bad cheque sentence, and that, in the period of a year, he had worked a total of four days at two jobs.

Mr Cooper: 'What did you do?'

Cody: 'I loafed.'

Mr Cooper: 'How did you support yourself?'

Cody: 'By my wit.'

Mr Cooper (later in reference to one of Cody's girl friends): 'Did she support you?'

Cody: 'Yes.'

Mr Cooper: 'Did she support you in Hollywood or did you live by your wits?'

Cody: 'Both.'

Mr Cooper: 'How about Las Vegas?'

Cody: 'I got a job as a shill at the Fremont Hotel—for two days.'

Mr Cooper: 'Was that very hard work?'

Cody: 'Oh, no. I was forced to quit. I had to get a police card. They would find out where I was and take me back to Minneapolis.'

Cooper became impatient with this frankness. Concerning the transaction with Dr Finch and Miss Tregoff he asked: 'You felt that, regardless of what the agreement had been, you had swindled Dr Finch and Carole?'

Cody: 'Well I don't know if I would call it swindled.'

Mr Cooper (sarcastically): 'Cheated?'

Cody (accepting the distinction): 'Yes.'

Mr Cooper tried another gambit. 'You wanted to co-oper-ate with the law enforcement officers. Was that out of the goodness of your heart?'

Cody: 'No, on the advice of my lawyer.'

Laughter in court. Mr Cooper turned in his hand.

Mr Egan also tried. He adopted the classical mode of attack. After a build-up based on the witness's lamentable record, he delivered what he hoped would be the *coup-de-grâce*.

'You've testified you've been hired to murder someone for money. Is that right?'

Cody: 'Yes, sir.'

Mr Egan: 'Would you lie for money?'

Mr Egan was silent. Cody thought about the question. Obviously he wanted to give a helpful, reasonable reply. Finally, he nodded. 'It looks like I have,' he said thoughtfully.

His meaning was plain. He meant that he had lied to get money out of Dr Finch and Miss Tregoff. There really was nothing to be done with the man.

With the departure of Cody (he returned to a cell in Minneapolis), the trial left the front pages for a bit. Asian flu and bronchitis claimed one of the male jurors, who was re-placed by a female alternative—seven women and five men were the arbiters now. Important witnesses were also ill. Miss Tregoff's attorneys scored a minor victory when they elimin-ated some of her self-incriminating statements from the record. There were scenes of jubilation and kisses were lavishly bestowed. But everyone knew that there were real charges for the pair to answer and that the only man who could answer them was Dr Finch.

As the moment approached when we would hear Grant Cooper outline the arguments for the defence, the tension rose. The queues waiting to occupy the seats reserved for the public lengthened. There was pushing and shoving. And not only in

3—A.T.K.

the corridor outside the courtroom. The press box became crammed. A San Francisco paper sent in a columnist noted for the trenchant advice he gave to his readers about the joys of mixed bathing in the nude. It was even rumoured, on the basis of the appearance in the press room of a tall, thin man with a bright blue suit and a long ginger beard, that the beatnik paper *Underhound* was covering the trial. Actresses with reporter's notebooks were two-a-penny.

On February 3, a month after the trial had begun, Cooper rose to address the jury.

The defence was that Dr Finch had lied steadily to Mrs Finch about his relationship with Miss Tregoff and that, until he had been served with the divorce papers in May, had believed that he had lied successfully.

When he learned that he had not, all his efforts had been bent to preventing a divorce, which would, he had feared, damage both his business prospects and his professional standing.

He had had two courses open to him. He could stall by pretending to want a reconciliation, or he could try to get evidence that his wife had been going with other men and was not, in fact, the innocent party she claimed to be.

He had tried to do both. When the reconciliation idea had not worked, he had employed private detectives to follow her. They had proved useless. They would follow her for a couple of hours and then lose her. And they had proved expensive. He had asked Miss Tregoff if there were not someone in Las Vegas who could do the work.

Dr Finch was also prepared to admit to discreditable behaviour. When Cody, whom he had hired to follow his wife, had suggested that, if it proved impossible to get other evidence against Mrs Finch, he himself should seduce her in order to provide it, the doctor had agreed dubiously that he could try. That had been all that Cody had been paid to do.

As for the alleged assaults on her, Dr Finch's case was that his wife had been a neurotic woman, who had imagined things and spread stories of his violence solely in order to substantiate her charges of cruelty in the divorce case. As for her being scared to death of guns, she had been able to hit a beer can at twenty feet with the very revolver that had killed her. In happier days, they had used it to practise target shooting on a hillside behind the house.

All in all, some very questionable behaviour; but murder, no.

On the day that the doctor was to give his evidence the corridor outside the courtroom became packed to suffocation. For once, the air-conditioning seemed ineffective. One elderly lady, who fainted in the queue, came to as she was being borne away and piped a despairing 'Hold my place.' Nobody did. Inside, things were scarcely better. Five visiting South Americans somehow managed to get into the press box. All credentials had to be checked before the interlopers could be identified and ejected. A columnist famed for her appearance on the 'What's My Line?' television programme was mobbed by autograph hunters. A woman juror got into a violent argument with one of the court sheriffs who refused to leave his post to get her book autographed. One cameraman was standing on the judge's desk to get a wider angle on the scene. The court was a little late in getting down to business; but in the end order was restored and the great moment came.

Dr Finch took the stand with the air of an experienced pilot taking over for an instrument landing in dense fog—tense but steady, nerves well under control. He asked at once if he could dispense with the microphone and rely upon the strength of his own voice to carry. 'If you can't hear me,' he instructed Cooper, 'hold up your hand.'

After Cooper had taken him through his account of the events leading up to the night of July 18, the doctor described what had happened at the house.

He had approached his wife in the garage saying that he wanted to talk to her. She had pulled out the gun. He had closed with her in order to take it away. She had fought with him. He had had to hit her with the gun—hence the skull fractures. When he had put the gun down (presumably to deal with the maid) she had snatched it back and started running down the driveway.

He did not know where Miss Tregoff was. He thought that his wife had seen her. He ran after his wife. When he caught up with her, she had the gun in her two hands (as she had always held it in target practice) and was pointing it—not at him but in a direction that could have meant that she had seen Miss Tregoff and was going to shoot her.

He grappled with her and there was a second struggle. As he again wrenched the gun away from her and started to throw it into the bushes, she started to run.

At that moment—he did not know how or why, or even if the gun had been cocked—the gun went off.

When he reached his wife, who was lying on the ground, he did not realise that she had been shot.

He said to her: 'What happened, Barbara? Where are you hurt?'

She said that she had been 'shot in the chest.'

'I told her not to move. I said, "I've got to get an ambulance for you and get you to the hospital." Barbara said, "Wait." She said, "I'm sorry, I should have listened." I said, "Barbara, don't talk about it now. I've got to get you to a hospital."'

At this point Dr Finch began to weep as he told the story.

'She said, "Don't leave me" and then she paused and said, "Take care of the kids."'

Dr Finch's voice broke and he had difficulty continuing.

'I checked her pulse right away. There was no pulsation. I turned up her chin. There was no respiration. She was dead.' And then he repeated it. 'She was *dead*. I said "Barb," but she couldn't answer.'

Dr Finch was not the only one weeping now. Some of the jurors were weeping with him.

But not all of them.

Cooper made the doctor act out the second struggle over the gun to show how it happened; but the demonstration did not really help.

Mrs Finch had been shot in the back and not at very close quarters. The doctor said that the gun had gone off as he had flung it away into the bushes. Could it have been defective? There was no way of knowing. The bushes had been searched and searched again. The gun had not been found, there or anywhere else.

The cross-examination of Dr Finch seemed curiously ineffectual. The first struggle in the garage was barely touched upon. Yet the doctor's own account of it contained some clear contradictions. If, as he claimed, his wife had had the gun and he had merely been trying to get it away from her, why had he not done just that? Why, when he had had the gun in his hand, had he *then* battered her about the head with it, and with sufficient force to fracture her skull in two places? And how had this woman (who must at least have been dazed by the blows) then managed to snatch up the gun, and run so fast down the driveway that he had only caught up with her when she had stopped and appeared to be aiming the gun?

The doctor's behaviour after the shooting seemed equally strange. Miss Tregoff said that she had hidden behind the bougainvillaea and remained there. Did her lover not try to

find her? Had he not even called to her? The grounds surrounding the house were not that extensive—little more than
an acre. Did he think that she had run away and left him to it?
There had been an easy way for him to find out. Her car, in
which they had driven down from Las Vegas, was in the
Country Club car park at the foot of the hill. He had had to
pass the Club in order to get to Citrus Avenue, where he had
stolen the Ford. Had he not looked to see if her car was still
there? We know it was because she drove back to Las Vegas in
it later. Therefore, she had had the keys. Rather than run the
risk of stealing a car, would it not have been easier to run back
up the hill and find her? Or were the approaching police car
sirens already audible?

Miss Tregoff's account was no less extraordinary. From her
hiding place she had heard screams, a shot, police cars and
policemen. If, as she said, Mrs Finch had had the gun, she
must have feared that the doctor had been shot. Yet she
claimed not to have known what had happened until she heard
it over the radio as she was driving back to Las Vegas.

It really was too much to swallow.

The admitted facts were that they had made their separate
ways back to Las Vegas. Even allowing for the conventional
panic after the accidental killing ('I didn't know *what* I was
doing!') the rest of the evidence looked remarkably like a
pathetic and ill-considered attempt to improvise an alibi for
Miss Tregoff.

When her evidence came to be heard it added nothing to
what the jury already knew. She just stuck to her story and
that was that.

Superior Judge Walter R. Evans summed up accurately and
fairly.

The jury deliberated for eight days and then announced that
they were unable to agree upon a verdict. Some of the jurors

were indiscreet enough to discuss the matter with the press later. They had been together for almost ten weeks and racial dissensions (the jury was not all-white) had, it appeared, led to ugly scenes in the jury room. The possibility of their agreeing about anything had been remote.

On June 28 a new trial was ordered.

It began, before Superior Judge LeRoy Dawson and a jury of eleven women and one man, on July 20. For the prosecution, this time, was Assistant District Attorney Crail. Mr Cooper again defended Dr Finch.

On October 19 the case went to the jury.

Twenty-four hours later, when it had become apparent that this jury, too, was unable to agree, Judge Dawson called them back into court and admonished them in startling terms.

He said that in his opinion they ought not to believe the evidence of Dr Finch and Miss Tregoff.

Cooper immediately protested. As the judge continued, Cooper interrupted constantly, and was twice told to be silent. Finally, he was cited for contempt of court.*

Brushing aside further protests, Judge Dawson now told the jury: 'The explanation given by the defendant, Dr Finch, as to the circumstances surrounding the firing of the fatal shot to me does not sound reasonable. In none of its aspects does it appear to me to have been anything but an attempt to justify what is shown by the evidence, in my opinion, to be a wilful and deliberate taking of human life.... To my mind the testimony given by the witness John Cody regarding the purpose for which he was employed was more believable than the testimony of the two defendants on the subject.'

* At the end of this trial he was fined $500. Later, the State of California set aside the conviction and reprimanded the judge.

But it was no good. After deliberating for a total of twenty days, the jury announced that they were unable to agree upon a verdict.

Dismissing them, Judge Dawson commented that, 'the failure of this jury to reach a verdict in this case raises a very disquieting question in the minds of all of us who are interested in the maintenance and functioning of the jury system.'

A third trial was ordered. It began on January 4, 1961, before Superior Judge David Coleman and a jury of ten men and two women. This time, Dr Finch was defended not by Mr Cooper in person, but by one of his associates.

The case went to the jury on March 23. Five days later they asked for the judge's guidance. Would there, they wanted to know, be any legal conflict in verdicts of guilty of first degree murder against one defendant, guilty of second degree murder against the other, and guilty of conspiracy against both?

The judge said that there would not.

The jury then brought in those verdicts: Dr Finch guilty of murder in the first degree, Miss Tregoff guilty of murder in the second degree, both guilty of conspiracy.

On the following week the jury reconvened to determine the sentences. After a further twelve hours of deliberation, they asked the judge if they could return a verdict of life imprisonment without the possibility of parole. He told them that the law did not permit the qualification.

Forty minutes later the jury determined sentences of life imprisonment for both defendants.

After dismissing motions by the defence for a new trial and modification of Miss Tregoff's sentence, Judge Coleman said: 'The jury's verdict speaks for itself. This was a brutal murder. There is no miscarriage of justice. The proof of their guilt is overwhelming.'

Both may apply for parole after serving seven years of their sentences.

Meanwhile, the doctor has had time for reflection. If Mrs Finch had lived to go through with the divorce suit he would have been stripped of most of his assets. As it was, he had to pay for his defence. The services of the best lawyers are never cheap. One day in September, 1959, at the jail, the doctor signed an agreement which was then lodged with the County Recorder.

In it, the doctor agreed to pay Mr Cooper a retainer of $25,000, plus $350 a day for each day of the trial in Superior Court. In order to cover these fees, the doctor assigned to Mr Cooper his assets in the West Covina Medical Center and its corporations, plus the deeds of his house, plus his cars and a twenty-two foot speedboat. Mr Cooper was empowered to sell what was necessary to pay his fees and expenses and hand back what remained afterwards. This fee arrangement covered the preparation of a motion for a new trial if that became necessary; but not the conduct of the case in any appelate court. If Mr Cooper were called upon to render further services to his client, fresh financial arrangements would have to be made. No doubt they were.

Perhaps Cody's mountain-top idea had not been so foolish after all.

3

James Hanratty

In August 1961, Mr Michael John Gregsten and Miss Valerie Storie were scientific workers on the staff of the Road Research Laboratory at Langley, near Slough in Buckinghamshire. Gregsten was a happily married man of thirty-four with two young children. Miss Storie was twenty-two and single. They were both members of the Laboratory staff motor club, and regularly took part in the club rallies.

Shortly before eight o'clock on the evening of Tuesday, August 22, they set out with maps and notebooks in Gregsten's car to survey the route of an eighty-mile rally which they were organising for the following Sunday. The car was a grey, four-door Morris Minor saloon.

Just after eight o'clock, they stopped briefly for a drink at the Old Station Inn, Taplow and then drove on along the route as far as Dorney Reach. There, they stopped just off the road by the edge of a cornfield. It was about 8.45 then and beginning to get dark. They had been there about twenty minutes, discussing the route and the timings and making their notes, when there was a tap on the window beside Gregsten.

What happened to the car and its occupants during the next ten hours was described by counsel at a hearing before the Ampthill Magistrates' Court in November. However, on that occasion Miss Storie's own evidence was heard *in camera*. This account is based on her evidence given at Bedfordshire Assizes in the following January.

She said that when Gregsten started to wind down the

window, the man outside who had tapped on the glass thrust a gun inside. He said: 'This is a hold-up. I am a desperate man. I have been on the run for four months. You do as I tell you, you will be all right.'

He then demanded the ignition key. Gregsten handed it over. The gunman locked the driver's door and got into the back of the car.

He kept talking. He said that he had not eaten for two days and that he had been sleeping out for the past two nights. He flourished the gun and remarked that he had not had it very long. 'This is like a cowboy's gun,' he added. 'I feel like a cowboy.'

Miss Storie thought the remark about sleeping out peculiar, because it had rained heavily the previous night and, as far as she could see, the man's clothes appeared 'immaculate.'

The gunman now returned the ignition key and told Gregsten to drive farther off the road into the field. Gregsten did so. The gunman then demanded their money and valuables. In the darkness, Miss Storie was able to remove most of the money from her handbag before handing it over.

The gunman went on talking. He complained again that he was hungry. In desperation they told him to take the car and the money and go—anything, if he would just leave them. He asked if there was something to eat in the car. Told that there wasn't, the gunman seemed to forget about food. He said, 'there's no hurry,' and added that every policeman in England was looking for him. He would wait until morning, then tie them up and leave.

To the wretched victims the whole thing must have been as bewildering as it was terrifying. They had given the man money and other valuables, they had offered to let him take the car and leave them stranded in the middle of a cornfield, they had tried to appease him in every way. But he did not seem to know *what* he wanted. In her evidence Miss Storie referred again and again to his indecision. The suggestion made later (though not by Miss Storie) that his sole motive from the beginning had been that of rape is difficult to accept. The confused behaviour is typical of a certain type of psychopath. It is probable that at that point he did not know what he meant to do.

The three had been sitting in the car for about an hour when a door in a near-by house opened. By the light inside they could see someone putting away a bicycle. The gunman became alarmed. 'If that man comes over here,' he told them, 'don't say anything. If you say anything, I will shoot him and then I will shoot you.'

Nobody came over, and after a while the gunman began talking again about being hungry. He could not stand it any longer, he said. He would go and find something to eat. He told Gregsten to get out, that he would drive. Gregsten, he decided, would be placed in the boot of the car.

Miss Storie's account of the arguments she had had to use in order to dissuade the gunman from putting this last proposal into practice is frightening. The Morris Minor is a well-designed car, but it is small. The very thought of cramming a fully grown man, alive, into the boot seems absurd. Yet, it was not until Miss Storie had declared desperately that there was a leak in the exhaust system and that the fumes from it would kill anyone placed in the boot, that the gunman could be persuaded to abandon the plan.

This grotesque discussion took place outside the car. It is interesting, not only for its high fantasy content, but because, *for the first time*, Miss Storie saw that the gunman had a folded handkerchief tied 'gangster fashion' over the lower part of his face. He had a Cockney accent she recalled. For 'things' and 'think,' he said 'fings' and 'fink.'

The gunman finally decided that he would return to the back seat and that Gregsten should drive, with the revolver at the back of his head to ensure that he followed the directions given.

The drive began. Directed by the gunman they went through Slough towards Stanmore. During this part of the drive, the gunman removed the handkerchief from his face, but warned Gregsten and Miss Storie to keep their eyes on the road ahead. Miss Storie said that she did not see his face clearly during the drive. He talked a lot, however. There was self-pity. He said that he had been in a remand home and that he had 'done the lot' and had never had a chance in life. There were friendly overtures. He returned their watches to them. Near London Airport, he told Gregsten to stop at a garage and gave him a pound note with which to buy petrol. There was a threepenny piece in the change. The gunman gave it to Miss Storie as a 'wedding present.' At Stanmore, he allowed Gregsten to stop and buy cigarettes from a vending machine. Miss Storie lighted cigarettes for Gregsten and herself, and handed one to the gunman behind them. As he took it, she noticed that he was wearing black gloves.

At Kingsbury the gunman directed them on to the A5 road to St Albans, and then on to the A6 road to Bedford. By then Gregsten had begun flashing the car's reversing light in an effort to attract attention of some passing motorist. He did succeed in making one driver slow down and point to the rear of the car. The gunman saw the signal and misunderstood it. He made Gregsten stop, and then checked that the rear lights were on. Miss Storie also said that Gregsten had managed to convey to her that he intended, if they saw a policeman, to turn the car up on to the pavement near him. However, during the drive, which covered forty-three miles, they saw no policeman.

The gunman, meanwhile, had forgotten his hunger and now

said that he needed somewhere to have a sleep. He would tie Gregsten and Miss Storie up first. At Deadman's Hill, on the A6 road at Clophill, near Luton, he saw a lay-by and told Gregsten to turn into it. Gregsten did so. When the car came to a standstill, he was told to switch off the lights.

There was some rope in the car. The gunman tied Miss Storie's wrists, not very securely, to a door handle. Earlier in the evening there had been a duffel bag full of laundry in the back of the car. The gunman had made them move it to the front. Now, he told Gregsten to pass it into the back seat. It may have been that he had decided to use the bag as a pillow. We don't know. As Gregsten heaved the bag over, the gunman shot him twice in the back of the head.

Gregsten fell forward and Miss Storie began to scream. The gunman told her to stop. Miss Storie said to him: 'You shot him, you bastard. Why did you do that?'

'He frightened me,' was the reply. 'He moved too quick. I got frightened.'

She could hear the blood pumping from the wounds in Gregsten's head. She pleaded with the gunman to get a doctor, or let her go for help. This produced more indecision. He replied: 'Be quiet, will you, I'm thinking.'

She went on pleading and he repeated the sentence. Then, he took a piece of the laundry in the duffel bag and put it over the dying man's face. As he did this, he said to Miss Storie: 'Turn round and face me. I know your hands are free.'

They were indeed free, and she had been trying to conceal the fact from him. Now, she turned and faced him.

He told her to kiss him. She refused.

At that moment, the headlights of a car passing on the road lit up the gunman's face.

'This,' Miss Storie said in her evidence, 'was the first opportunity of really seeing what he looked like. He had very large, pale blue, staring icy eyes. He seemed to have a pale face. I should imagine anyone should have, having just shot someone. He had jet brown hair, combed back with no parting. The light was only on his face for a few seconds as the vehicle went past, then we were in complete darkness again.'

Miss Storie admitted that her vision was poor without glasses; but, at that moment, she was wearing her glasses and could see well.

The gunman now forced her to kiss him. She noted that he was clean shaven.

He then ordered her to get into the back of the car with him. When she refused, he threatened to shoot her. 'I will count five. If you haven't got in, I will shoot.'

She got in. He threatened her again, made her take some clothing off, and then raped her. Her revulsion seemed to amuse him. 'You haven't had much sex, have you?' he said when it was over.

He now made her help him drag Gregsten's body out of the front seat, and show him how to start the car. He seemed about to drive off. She went to Gregsten's body, which was lying on the concrete of the lay-by a few yards away.

The gunman got out of the car and came over to her. He said: 'I think I had better hit you in the head or something to knock you out, or else you will go for help.'

Miss Storie promised that she would not do so and implored him to go. She gave him one of the pound notes she had previously hidden.

The gunman started to walk away, then suddenly turned and began shooting. He fired four shots at her, then reloaded the gun and fired six more. Of the ten shots, five hit her. One bullet lodged in the spine and paralysed her legs.

When the gunman moved her with his foot, she feigned death. Finally, he drove away.

It would have been understandable if, after the nightmare hours she had already lived through, Miss Storie had lost all ability to think. Yet, wounded and paralysed though she was, she realised that if she died, there would be no witness to what had happened. She tried to write a description of the gunman by forming letters with small stones on the concrete—'blue eyes and brown hair.' She failed because there were not enough stones within her reach; she could not move to get more. She called for help, but none came. She lay there with the dead Gregsten for the remainder of the night. At 6.40 in the morning, a labourer on his way to work heard her call and went for help.

The hunt for the gunman began. Detective Superintendent Acott of Scotland Yard took charge of the investigation.

That same day, a man telephoned the police and reported that the missing car was abandoned in Avondale Crescent, Ilford, forty-two miles from the final scene of the crime. The informant gave a name and address which later proved to be false; but the car was where he had said it was, and the seats were still bloodstained.

The following day, a cleaner working in the bus garage at Rye Lane in South London found a loaded ·38 Enfield revolver and five boxes of ammunition under the rear seat of a 36A bus. Tests soon established that this was the murder weapon.

Miss Storie was in Bedford General Hospital in a critical condition and several days elapsed before she was able to amplify the first brief statements she had made to the police. On August 29, however, Scotland Yard issued two portraits built up with her help on the Identi-kit system.

Identi-kit is an American device, now widely used in criminal investigation. It consists of hundreds of transparencies each embodying a different facial characteristic. By means of superimposition, a witness's description is gradually translated into a visual statement which can be photographed.

After publication of the pictures, a number of men answering the description were questioned by Scotland Yard. Some four weeks later, on September 24, an identification parade was held in a ward at Guy's Hospital, where Miss Storie was now recuperating after an operation to remove two of the bullets from a lung.

Among those in the parade was a man who bore a marked resemblance to one of the Identi-kit portraits, and who was about to be charged with causing 'grievous bodily harm' to another woman.

Miss Storie did not identify that man at the parade, though, in a discussion with a doctor and the police afterwards, she agreed that there might be a resemblance. During the parade, she had picked out another man known to be innocent.

On October 6, a man calling himself Jimmy Ryan telephoned Superintendent Acott at Scotland Yard.

The man's real name was James Hanratty. He was twenty-five years old and already well known to the police. At school he had been considered unteachable. At fifteen he could neither read nor write. In 1952, an episode of amnesia had ended in his being diagnosed, after psychiatric examination in an institution, as a mental defective. He had become a burglar. At nineteen he had received further psychiatric treatment. The following year, while in prison, he had made a suicide attempt. Prison psychiatrists had described him then as a potential psychopath. During the months preceding the murder, he had burgled a number of houses in the Stanmore–Harrow area.

In his telephone conversation with Superintendent Acott, Hanratty said that he had heard that the police suspected him. He went on: 'I want to talk to you and clear up this whole thing, but I cannot come in there. I am very worried and don't know what to do. I know you are the only one who can help me. . . . I know I have left my fingerprints at different places, and done different things, and the police want me. But I want to tell you, Mr Acott, that I did not do that A6 murder.'

The Superintendent tried to keep him talking, but Hanratty had had enough.

'I'm so upset I don't know what I'm doing and what I'm saying,' he declared; 'I've got a very bad head and suffer from blackouts and lose my memory. Look I will have to go now and think it over.'

The Superintendent tried again to persuade him to come in and make a statement. Hanratty hesitated.

'I will phone you tonight between ten and twelve and tell you what I have decided,' he replied. 'I must go now. My head's bad and I've got to think.'

He pronounced the word 'think' as 'fink,' as do a great many other Londoners.

Hanratty, again using the name Ryan, next called a newspaper, explained his problem to an assistant news editor and asked for advice. He said that he had an alibi for the night of the murder, that he had in fact been in Liverpool at the time with business friends, but that he could not involve them. The inference was that the business on which they had been engaged had been criminal. The news editor advised him to go to the police.

Superintendent Acott received a second telephone call. It was as unproductive as the first. Hanratty ended it by saying: 'Now I must go, Mr Acott. I want to talk to you but you will catch me. I am going, Mr Acott.'

The following day he telephoned yet again, this time from Liverpool.

He said that the three friends who could prove his alibi for the night of the murder refused to help him. 'You can't blame them because they are fences. You know what I mean, they receive jewellery. . . . I don't know what to do. . . .'

The Superintendent said that he would have to have some corroboration from witnesses and asked for the names of the three men. Hanratty refused to give the names.

Five days later he was arrested in Blackpool. Again he refused to give the names of the three men. The Superintendent warned him of the seriousness of his position and told him that two empty cartridge cases had been found in a hotel room he had occupied on the night before the murder.*

Hanratty considered that this last fact completely cleared him, because, 'I told you I have never had any bullets and never fired a gun.' He appeared to feel that a simple denial on his part ought to be enough. As to the need for corroborative evidence of his whereabouts on the night of the murder, he said: 'I am a very good gambler, Mr Acott. I have gambled all my life. I am going to gamble now. I am not going to name the three men. I can get out of this without them.'

He was mistaken.

On the morning after the murder two motorists in the Ilford area had noticed a grey Morris Minor being driven erratically and dangerously. One of the motorists had been sufficiently incensed to shout at the driver of the Morris; both had been close enough to see his face. At an identity parade both identified Hanratty. On the other hand, a passenger in one of the cars, who recalled that the driver of the Morris had had a 'horrible smile,' attended two identity parades and picked out a different man each time, neither of them Hanratty.

Miss Storie had by then been moved to the spinal injuries centre at Stoke Mandeville Hospital for further treatment.

* The Superintendent did not tell him, however, that the cartridge cases were of .38 calibre and had been related by tests to the murder weapon.

On October 14 yet another identification parade was held. There were thirteen men in the parade, Hanratty among them.

On this occasion, Miss Storie asked that each man be told to say the sentence, 'Be quiet will you, I'm thinking.' After fifteen or twenty minutes, she identified Hanratty.

The following day he was charged with the murder of Gregsten.

His trial began at Bedfordshire Assizes on January 22, and lasted twenty-two days.

James Hanratty may or may not have been a mental defective in the medical sense of the term; he may or may not have been a psychopath; he was, without a doubt, a deeply stupid man. If he was guilty—and most probably he was—he made the prosecution's task easier than it need have been. If he was innocent, he made his own counsel's task infinitely more difficult, and contributed handsomely to his own destruction.

His story about the three men in Liverpool, whose names he knew and who could if they chose give him an alibi, was a lie. But he went on telling it after his arrest. He told it to his solicitor, and he told it to his defending counsel. He told it after the Magistrates' Court hearing and his committal. It was not until early in February, after he had heard the prosecution's case at his trial, that he let his legal advisers know that he had been deceiving them. He said that on the night in question he had really stayed in a bed-and-breakfast house at Rhyl in North Wales.

In the witness box, he explained himself this way: 'I didn't tell Superintendent Acott, because at that point I did not know the name of the street, the number of the house, or even the name of the people in the house. At that stage I knew that I was only wanted for interviewing, not for the actual A6 murder charge, which I found out later, or the truth would have been told straight away. I know I made a terrible mistake by telling Superintendent Acott about these three men, but I have been advised that the truth only counts in this matter, and might I say here every word of that is the truth.'

His counsel then asked him: 'Will you explain to my Lord and the jury why it was that after telling Mr Acott this story you persisted in it for so long?'

'Because, my Lord, I am a man with a prison record,' was the answer; 'and I know that in such a trial as this it is very vital for a man once to change his evidence in such a serious trial. But I know inside of me, somewhere in Rhyl this house does exist, and by telling the truth these people will come to my assistance.'

Thanks to prompt and energetic inquiries made by the defence team, a Rhyl landlady was found who thought she remembered him. She 'felt' that he had stayed at her house on or about the date in question. She could not be certain though, and could not produce her visitors' book for that time as it had been destroyed.

However, Hanratty did not *have* to prove an alibi. His defence was that they had the wrong man. The prosecution's case for having the right man rested on Miss Storie's identification of him at the parade of October 14, the identification of the two motorists, and on very little else. Prosecution efforts to connect him with the murder weapon, through the cartridge cases found in the hotel, were frustrated when the hotel manager, upon whose evidence the police had relied, proved to be a man with a long criminal record who admitted that he had lied in order to 'help' the police, and also confused Hanratty with another man.

With the annihilation of this witness the defence may well have felt that they were making headway. If so, they had reckoned without their client.

On the eighth day of the trial, the prosecution called upon a rather odd type of man to give evidence. He was twenty-four, and had, he readily admitted, a criminal record.

In November of the previous year he had been in Brixton Prison awaiting trial on a fraud charge. Hanratty had also been in the prison on remand at that time. The witness said that they had spoken to one another in the exercise yard on a number of occasions. Eventually, he said, Hanratty had told him that he (Hanratty) was the A6 killer, and had spoken of Miss Storie and how he had raped her. According to the ex-convict, Hanratty had also said that he was 'sort of choked' that Miss Storie was living, as she was the only witness against him.

The defence, of course, claimed that it was all a pack of lies. In his summing-up, the Judge advised the jury to approach this evidence 'with care.' It is possible to believe the ex-convict's story nevertheless. A man of Hanratty's mentality would be quite capable of telling a fellow prisoner that he was the 'A6 killer' simply in order to make himself seem important.

Certainly, the jury did not find Hanratty's an easy case to decide. They were out almost ten hours. After six hours of deliberation, they sent a letter to the Judge requesting additional guidance. Its content is significant.

'May we have a further statement from you regarding the definition of reasonable doubt. Would you confirm that we judge the case on reasonable doubt, or must we be certain sure of the prisoner's guilt to return a verdict?

'Will you please also comment on the summing-up quoted by defence counsel, with a special reference to circumstantial evidence on the previous case, and the bearing on this case with regard to identification and the cartridge cases found at the Vienna Hotel?

'Would you please comment on the point made that when there is circumstantial evidence which admits of more than one theory, then the theory in favour of the defence must invariably be adopted?'

The jury returned to court to hear the Judge's reply.

He reminded them that he had said that they must be 'sure,' and went on: 'Well, if you have a reasonable doubt, not a mere fancy sort of doubt, if you have a reasonable doubt you cannot be sure.'

On the question of identification, he said: 'You have to be quite sure that the evidence of identification was such that you, and each of you, can feel sure that, as a result of that identification, it was the prisoner that has been identified.'

Hanratty was found guilty, and in April he was hanged.

There was, and is, no reasonable doubt that he was guilty. But when we are taking the irreversible step of executing a man, should there be *any* permissible kind of doubt, even the 'mere fancy' kind?

Well, doubtless there has to be. Otherwise, nobody would *ever* be executed.

The
Lizzie Borden
Memorial Lectures

1

England

People begin to see that something more goes to the composition of a fine murder than two block-heads to kill and be killed—a knife—and a dark lane. Design, gentlemen, grouping, light and shade, poetry, sentiment are now deemed indispensable to attempts of this nature.

On Murder as a Fine Art
THOMAS DE QUINCEY

Ladies and gentlemen, little more than a century has passed since Thomas de Quincey wrote those oft-quoted words. Yet, to the modern student of murder, steeped in the tradition of William Roughead, Edmund Pearson, William Bolitho and Christopher Morley, they already have a platitudinous ring.

Yes, we have come a long way; and British students have not been slow to recognise the debt they owe to American scholarship. Nevertheless, it has seemed to some of us in Britain that, in spite of the great erudition and high sensibility of the post-Woollcott school of American murder-fanciers (or, perhaps, because of them?), their insights have remained to some extent limited. When, therefore, the President of the Incorporated Society of American Murder-Tasters asked me, an Englishman, to deliver the Lizzie Borden Memorial Lectures for this year, I had no difficulty in choosing a theme.

Ladies and gentlemen, our Anglo-Saxon culture is built on studious denials of the existence within us of the primitive. The revelation that there is, after all, an ape beneath the velvet is perennially fascinating. Surely, that is why we so value a good murder. Where you, my American friends, seem to have gone astray (and I offer the suggestion in all humility) is in your tendency to concentrate your interest and researches on the ape, to the virtual exclusion of the velvet. The two must be complementary. What the murderer said to his victim as he slipped the antimony into the cocoa is undeniably important; but how can we assess the full emotional flavour of the situation (to say nothing of that of the cocoa) without also considering the *actual building in which the crime was hatched and committed*?

I do not pretend that my interest in this important facet of murder-study is a recent development. In fact, it originated in a disturbing emotional experience of my adolescence.

On Saturday, April 12, 1924, a young man named Patrick Mahon entered a London hardware store and bought a meat-saw and a cook's ten-inch knife. Thus equipped, he went to Waterloo Station, picked up a suitcase he had checked there, and took a train to Eastbourne, a town on the Sussex coast of the English Channel.

Between Eastbourne and Pevensey Bay is a desolate area of shingle and sand dunes known locally as the Crumbles; and here, in a small cottage which he had rented a few days earlier, a Miss Emily Kaye awaited him. She was a stenographer whom he had met in London; and this was to be the beginning of a two months' 'love experiment' (to use Mahon's own limpid phrase) which would, if it proved successful, make way for a more permanent relationship.

At least, that was Miss Kaye's understanding of the situation, and she had demonstrated her optimistic view of it by

selling some bonds she owned and giving her lover the proceeds. His feelings about the future were undoubtedly different. On the following Tuesday he strangled her, dismembered
her body, packed the pieces tightly into some old boxes, and
returned to London.

From the point of view of the serious murder-fancier it was
not a particularly distinguished crime. There was no mystery
about it, and, in spite of the newspapers' efforts, precious little
of the macabre. No special detective skill was needed to bring
the murderer to book. No doubts exercised the jury. Patrick
Mahon was a commonplace psychotic who had already served
a five-year prison sentence for assault.

However, distinguished or no, it was the first real murder
case in which I had taken an interest. A lad of fifteen, I had
just read Dostoevski's *Crime and Punishment* and been shattered by it. Wrapped in the mantle of Raskolnikov, I used to
go for long, gloomy walks in the more depressing quarters of
London, looking for fallen women whom I could salute,
though from a respectable distance, in the name of suffering
humanity.

The family holiday that year took us to a resort within
cycling distance of Eastbourne and, three days before Mahon
was hanged, I decided to ride over there, visit the Crumbles
and inspect the celebrated cottage. Through solitary commun-
ion with the scene of the crime, I felt that I might come to
closer grips with the problems of good and evil with which my
anxiety-laden mind was preoccupied.

Judge, then, my horror, my disgust, my indignation, when I
found the whole site cluttered with morbid sight-seers, and the
murder cottage itself practically torn to pieces by souvenir-
hunting vandals!

The incident made an unforgettable impression on me.
When the London County Council initiated the system of

marking those houses which possess literary, artistic or other historical association with blue commemorative plaques, it was I who proposed that distinguished murder houses be marked with red plaques. My proposal was ignored. Some people seem to have no sense at all of historical responsibility. No sooner is a distinguished murder committed than they are agitating for the street name to be changed or the houses to be renumbered.

Happily, these ill-natured attempts are not often successful. The classic instance of a failure to distort history in this way is, of course, supplied by the English town of Rugeley in Staffordshire, home of Dr William Palmer, probably the most distinguished poisoner of all time. Palmer certainly poisoned at least fourteen persons for money, and although only three of the murders were proved against him at his trial in 1856, the case aroused enormous public interest. One might suppose that Rugeley would have been proud of Palmer; but no. Soon after the trial a craven group of citizens actually petitioned the Prime Minister of England for permission to change the town's name.

Fortunately, the Prime Minister was a man of wit and also a keen murder-taster. He readily gave the permission, but with the proviso that the town should be renamed after him. His name was Palmerston. Rugeley's name remained Rugeley.

As you may imagine, the World War II years brought additional anxieties. And some bitterness too. When other national treasures were being moved to safe places in the country, it was heart-breaking to find that *no special steps whatsoever* were being taken to protect such famous London buildings as 63 Tollington Park, and the left luggage office at Charing Cross Station* from enemy attack.

They survived, of course, but only thanks to Providence. I well remember my despair on hearing that the Camden Road

* The trunk murderer's home from home.

area of London had been badly hit in a night bombing and that the immortal 39 (now 30) Hilldrop Crescent was a hole in the ground. I was away in the army at the time and could not check this terrible report. In fact it was not until I came to do the field work for this very survey that I learned that, although the bombs had fallen very close to Dr Crippen's former home, and although the damage to neighbouring property had been severe, the old place itself still stood; a little shabby, perhaps, a little run down, but still proudly intact.

It was a moving discovery. Britain and America have many cultural ties; but what could be a more enduring emotional link between our two democracies than the basement of 39 Hilldrop Crescent?

Dr Hawley Harvey Crippen was the son of a dry-goods merchant in Coldwater, Michigan. He studied medicine at the Homeopathic Hospital College of Cleveland, Ohio, and took his diploma as an eye and ear specialist at the Ophthalmic Hospital in New York. As American as they come. After the death of his first wife in 1891 (from natural causes) in Salt Lake City, he went to New York. There he met a girl of seventeen, Kunigunde Mackamotzki (father Polish, mother German), who called herself Cora Turner. She was living at the time with a man named C. C. Lincoln. In 1893 she became the second Mrs Crippen.

A great deal has been written about the insignificant-looking, myopic little doctor with his sandy moustache, his gold-rimmed spectacles, his high, domed forehead, his apologetic manner. He has been, too, the archetype of many a medically qualified fictional murderer. Let us look, for a moment, at Miss Mackamotzki.

She was a robust, handsome brunette-turned-blonde with dark, heavily-lidded eyes and a manner which all who knew her described as 'lively.' She had heavy demands to make upon the man of her choice. To begin with, he must patronise her ambition to become a professional singer by paying teachers to foster her non-existent talent, composers to write songs for her, and agents to offer her services to unresponsive managements. He must also, of course, pay for her clothes; no ordinary liability since she believed that her inability to get professional engagements was somehow due to the inadequacies of her wardrobe, and every setback was followed by an orgy of dress buying. To complete the picture, it must be said that she was a full-blooded girl whose carnal needs were as excessive as her financial ones. Lively, indeed! C. C. Lincoln must have sighed with relief when she left him.

Towards the end of 1899, the doctor obtained a job with a patent-medicine manufacturer and was sent to England to manage the London office. Four months later Cora joined him. It was not until 1905 that they moved to Hilldrop Crescent.

The intervening years had not dealt kindly with either of them. We can learn about the state of their relationship from the interior arrangements of the house at that time.

The walls were painted a florid pink, Mrs Crippen's lucky colour, and, owing to her dislike of ventilation, the place smelled. The four upper rooms were occupied by lodgers and the Crippens lived mostly in the basement. At six every morning the doctor would get up to clean the lodgers' shoes, light the fires and make breakfast for all before leaving for his office. On his return at night he would help with supper. Mrs Crippen appropriated the rent money for her dress allowance. The household bills were paid by the doctor.

Soon after she arrived in England, Cora Crippen took the stage name of Belle Elmore and set out to conquer London music hall audiences. She flopped abysmally, and at the last of her two or three isolated appearances was booed off the stage. After that, she cultivated the fiction that she had retired from the stage after a long, successful career. She read the stage papers, bought expensive clothes and joined an artistes' benevolent association, The Music Hall Ladies' Guild. The ladies of the Guild found her gay and generous; 'lively,' in fact. At home she was a slattern and a scold.

Crippen bore his troubles with remarkable patience and restraint. He knew, because she had told him, that his wife was unfaithful to him. Yet, in spite of everything—her meanness at home, her wild extravagance outside, her selfishness and her shrill outbursts of nagging—he remained quietly subservient to her; until January, 1910.

The problem of how this mother-fixated masochist could suddenly turn into a wilful murderer has always been a tantalising one.

The most popular theory nowadays seems to be that he did not turn into a wilful murderer, but that he killed his wife accidentally. Having fallen in love with his secretary, Miss Ethel Le Neve, the story goes, and being unable to meet the double demands upon his virility, he recalls from his medical studies that nymphomania is treated with hyoscin hydrobromide. Thereupon, he doses his wife with the stuff, misjudges the quantity and kills her. He then panics, dismembers the body and buries it under the basement floor.

Unhappily, this engaging explanation is contradicted by the evidence. Firstly, the Crippens had been sleeping in separate rooms for years. Secondly, the dose of hyoscin he administered was ten times the maximum prescribed in the pharmacopoeia, a book with which he was certainly familiar. Thirdly, his behaviour immediately after the murder (for example, he gave Miss Le Neve some pieces of Mrs Crippen's jewellery to wear in public) suggests not panic but a ghastly self-confidence. The panic flight aboard the S.S. *Montrose* came later.

4—A.T.K.

Personally, I prefer a more old-fashioned explanation. Crippen fell in love with Miss Le Neve and told Cora he wanted a divorce. As a devout Catholic, she refused. It was the last straw. When he is really in love for the first time in his life, even a mother-fixated, masochistic worm can turn.

It was a wet, January day when I last inspected the house; the anniversary, it so happened, of the purchase of the hyoscin. After ten minutes of Hilldrop Crescent in the wet, almost any explanation of the crime would seem credible. The visiting student is advised to take a raincoat and to keep his taxi waiting.

In fact, the same taxi might well take him on hurriedly to the next London murder home on his list. Leaving Holloway Prison on his left, and travelling in the general direction of Finsbury, five minutes' driving will bring him to Tollington Park, Islington, a street as straight as a hangman's rope, and, in the rain, about as cheerful. The significant house is Number 63. The significant name is that of Seddon, the poisoner.

Ladies and gentlemen, when I first mentioned the theme of these lectures to a British colleague, I had to listen to some most ill-natured criticism. Did I really suppose, he sneered, that the frame was as important as the picture? Was I proposing to claim a relationship between certain styles of architecture and the impulse to murder? Or was this merely an arch lapse into the pathetic fallacy, the anthropomorphic ah-if-these-stones-could-only-speak sort of rubbish?

I will not mention the man's name. Since his prosecution on a charge of attempting to steal the door knocker from 10 Rillington Place,* and after the magistrate's timely denunciation of vulgar, sensation-mongering souvenir hunters, little has been heard of him, and he must be held discredited. I

---

* Bus or tube to Notting Hill Gate, then walk. Since this lecture was delivered, the name of Rillington Place has been changed to Ruston Close.

would only add that if any visiting student cares to explore the subject of English murder-home architecture he can count on my encouragement and guidance. He might well start with Tollington Park.

Frederick Henry Seddon was the district superintendent for an insurance company when he bought Number 63. That was in 1909; and in November of that year he brought his wife, his father and his five children to live there. He was forty; a good business-man, shrewd and hardworking; but with an obsessional attitude towards money and property that verged on the pathological. He rented the basement of the house as an office to his employers. He partitioned one of the upper rooms so that it could accommodate his father, the maidservant and four of the children. The top floor he decided to lease unfurnished. In July, 1910, he found a tenant, a middle-aged spinster named Eliza Mary Barrow.

She was an unhappy creature. A quarrelsome alcoholic with a small private income, derived from property and some gilt-edged securities she had inherited, she had accumulated during her stormy progress from lodging to lodging a retinue consisting of a couple named Hook, who acted as her servants in exchange for their bed and board, and an eight-year-old orphan named Ernie Grant. She was miserly in the picture-book sense of the word—she used to keep gold coins and count them—deeply distrusted banks, and was perpetually fearful of some disaster which would depreciate her capital. One day she sought the business-like Seddon's advice on the subject.

It was like dangling a hunk of fresh meat before a hungry tiger.

The first thing that happened was that the Hooks were given notice to quit by Seddon, acting on Miss Barrow's behalf. By October, 1910, Seddon had persuaded Miss Barrow to devote her capital to the purchase of an annuity—from Seddon personally.

It is not clear just when Seddon decided that he would have to murder Miss Barrow. All we know is that it was not until August of the following year that he sent his daughter Maggie to buy some arsenical flypapers. As this purchase was part of his plan to suggest that the victim had absorbed arsenic accidentally, the decision must have been made some days earlier; probably towards the end of July. By then, he had had Miss Barrow's capital in his hands for over six months, and for over six months he had been paying out the annuity. To him, it must have seemed monstrously unfair that he should have to go on doing so. After all, where was the profit in selling an annuity if the buyer were not soon to die?

So, in September, after a two weeks' illness in the top floor front bedroom, she died. A doctor certified the death as due to 'epidemic diarrhoea and exhaustion.' She was buried cheaply and hurriedly in a common grave. The funeral cost £3. Seddon demanded from the undertaker, and received, a small commission on the deal.

Unfortunately for Seddon, Miss Barrow had relatives, and although she had quarrelled with them repeatedly, they always in the end had made friendly overtures. No doubt the fact that she had an estate to bequeath helped. At all events, a few days after the funeral, relatives bent on reconciliation arrived at Tollington Park. To their consternation they found not merely that Miss Barrow was dead, but that Seddon was the executor of a will leaving what remained of her estate to Ernie Grant.

Within two months of the funeral the police had been induced to interest themselves in the affair, an exhumation order had been obtained, and arsenic found in the body. In March, 1912, Seddon and his wife were tried for murder.

It was one of the great arsenic trials. Counsel on both sides were brilliant. So was Seddon. He was in the witness box for two days and for over half the time was being rigorously cross-examined by the Attorney-General. He did not crack. The case against him was by no means strong, and he had a logical, intelligent and reasonable answer for everything. Yet he still managed to convince the jury that he was a murderer, and that his wife was absolutely innocent. What he did, in fact, was to reveal his monstrous obsession with money so blatantly that by the time he had finished he was regarded with loathing by everyone in court. 'Never,' one onlooker is reported to have said, 'have I seen a soul stripped as naked as that.' Seddon himself was apparently quite unaware of the impression he had created. He went to the gallows a very indignant man.

Number 63 is in excellent condition and the brickwork appears to have been repointed fairly recently. Seddon would have approved.

But, ladies and gentlemen, I think that it is time to leave London for the fresh air of the country and the seashore. Where shall we go? Herne Bay? I regret to inform you that the 80 High Street which saw George Joseph Smith's first bride-drowning is no longer there, the site being occupied by a chintzy restaurant called The Pantry; while the plumbing emporium next door but one, which carries a big display of baths, is not Hill's, the ironmonger's from which the famous bath was purchased. A pity.

His next murder was in Blackpool, also by the sea. Yet here again I have been disappointed. Blackpool is full of boarding houses, but that belonging to the late Mrs Crossley of Regent Road (the Mrs Crossley who angrily shouted 'Crippen!' after the newly-bereaved but complacent Smith) has eluded me. In fact, Smith's traces seem to have been completely covered. His last murder, at Miss Blatch's boarding house in Bismarck

Road, Highgate, is also without its memorial; Bismarck Road no longer exists.

If I have so far dealt mainly with poisoners, it is not because I scorn the less devious practitioners of murder. My difficulty is that so many of the more violent murders have been committed out of doors. Again, in many of these cases the murderer is only an incidental protagonist. It is the victim or a third party who is the nub of the matter; or even society itself. So it seemed to me the other day as I stood looking at the Villa Madeira in Bournemouth.

In 1934, foolish, sad, oversexed Mrs Rattenbury (37) hired muscular, dim-witted George Stoner (17) as chauffeur. Soon he became her lover. A few months later, in a fit of infantile jealousy, he took a mallet to the husband, bibulous, inoffensive Mr Rattenbury (67), and killed him. Mrs Rattenbury attempted to take the blame, and was tried with Stoner for the murder. She was acquitted. He was convicted and sentenced to death. His sentence was later commuted to life imprisonment; but Mrs Rattenbury never knew that. Soon after her acquittal, she committed suicide.

At the time, the case aroused a great deal of moral indignation. Alma Rattenbury was virtually driven to suicide. Before stabbing herself to death on the bank of a river near Christchurch, she wrote a note which ended: 'Thank God for peace at last.'

The house in which her tragedy was acted out is still there, though it is no longer called Villa Madeira. Let us leave that in peace, too. There is nothing there for the murder-taster. He prefers to believe in justice.

A visit to Wales will cheer us up. Let us go over the English border to Cusop Dingle, near the town of Hay-on-Wye.

There, in 1919, in a house called *Mayfield*, there lived Major Herbert Rowse Armstrong, his wife Katherine and their three children. The husband was not as martial a figure as his title might suggest. He was under-sized, ingratiating and hen-pecked.

Katherine was a formidable woman. She forbade alcohol and smoking in the house and if her husband were offered a drink at a neighbour's he had to have her permission before accepting. Usually, permission was withheld. She had a lively sense of discipline. Once, at a tennis party, she loudly ordered the major home because it was his 'bath night.'

In 1920 she was certified insane and removed to an asylum for treatment. In January, 1921, she returned to *Mayfield*, and the major, who had liked the taste of freedom, bought some arsenic. In February he administered it. She had been ill with nephritis and a heart disease, and the local doctor certi-fied her death as due to natural causes following an attack of gastritis. The major had got away with murder; and the fact went to his head.

An interesting character this; probably the nearest approach to a fictional murderer there has been. Having attained free-dom, he developed a taste for power. After the death of his wife and a period of dalliance in Italy, he returned to his house in Cusop, a new and dangerous man. He had realised that all he had to do to dispose of someone he did not like was to give that person a pinch of arsenic.

It is not known exactly how many persons he dosed, but it is certain that quite a number of those who accepted his hospital-ity during the latter part of 1921 (including the local Income Tax Inspector) afterwards became very sick with symptoms of arsenic poisoning, and one, at least, died of it. One who did not die was a Mr Martin.

Major Armstrong was a solicitor with an office in the main street of Hay. On the opposite side of the street in another office sat Mr Martin, also a solicitor, and the major's only competitor in town. In October a dispute arose between the two men over a property sale and Mr Martin demanded the repayment of his client's deposit. The major's reply was to ask Mr Martin to tea at *Mayfield* to discuss the matter. Mr Martin ate a buttered scone and was in bed for four days with an illness that the doctor (who was by now becoming familiar with the symptoms) diagnosed as arsenic poisoning. The authorities were informed.

A macabre little comedy was now enacted. The police, afraid to do anything that would arouse the major's suspicions before they had built up their case, bound the doctor and Mr Martin to secrecy. The major, on the other hand, having failed to dispose of Mr Martin the first time, was determined to try again. He proceeded to bombard Mr Martin with invitations to tea.

The wretched Martin had an appalling two months. He had had one painful dose of arsenic and did not want another. Yet, if he rejected the major's invitations without reasonable excuses, that terrible little man's suspicions might be aroused. The major changed his tactics and issued an invitation to dinner. Then, when Martin and his wife were at breaking point, the police acted. The major was arrested. Arsenic, wrapped in handy little packets, was found in his pockets. The exhumation of Mrs Armstrong's body followed. Five months later the major was hanged.

Ladies and gentlemen, at the beginning of this lecture I suggested that it was the revelation of the primitive beneath the mundane that made murder interesting to us. Yet, is that, after all, the whole story?

Looking back over the distinguished murderers in this present list, it seems to me that those who retain our interest (and, if I may say so, our affection) have two things in common. They murdered for severely practical reasons—profit, security, freedom—without feelings of guilt.

Perhaps we envy them. The murders we commit in our hearts can never be as simple.

2

Scotland

Ladies and gentlemen, in the first of these lectures, I ventured to criticise my countrymen for their failure to memorialise and, where possible, to preserve their historic murder buildings.

Needless to say, the British reaction has been apathetic. The warmth of the American response has been consequently all the more gratifying; in some respects, even a trifle disconcerting.

Thomas M. McDade, corresponding secretary of the American Society of Connoisseurs in Murder (if you will forgive my mentioning a rival body) is particularly forthright.

'Murder,' he writes, 'is in the public domain. Eventually, British Officialdom will no doubt see the wisdom of preserving their scenes of homicide, which are more a part of the national heritage than many a country estate or Norman fief.' He also takes a look into the future. 'It is said that the murderer feels compelled to return to the scene of the crime. In this he shares an impulse with millions. In time we may hope that he can indulge this compulsion by paying his shilling (or quarter) and joining a properly conducted tour to hear a guide explain how he (the murderer) did it.'

Letters inquiring wistfully after particular buildings have been numerous. Typical is the one from Mr Carl D. Halbak of Buffalo, New York, who is anxious about the sinister Moat

House Farm, where the monstrous Dougal did away with poor
Mrs Holland, and the boarding house which figured in the
Camden Town murder. Such letters are surely evidence
enough of that lively interest in murder for its own sake so
characteristic of a vigorous and ascendant culture.

In one respect, however, I have misled my American colleagues. I referred to 'British' indifference and to 'British'
obscurantism on the subject. For this reckless solecism, I
apologise. I should have said 'English.'

How different, indeed, is the attitude in Scotland!

Of course, Scottish murder has always had a special full-
bodied flavour of its own; burgundy to the English claret.
Perhaps it is something in the soil of Scotland; perhaps it is
something in their laws. Where else can you find expressed
such manifest and magnificent ambivalence towards the murderer as in the Scottish legal verdict of 'Not Proven'? Let the
envious English (or American) purist object that an accused
person is either guilty or not guilty and that the Not Proven
verdict merely permits a jury of palterers to hedge. The Scots
know a good murder mystery when they see it, and are good-
naturedly reluctant to punish the author if they can reasonably
avoid doing so. As Miss Tennyson Jesse suggests, the verdict
of Not Proven is an admonition: 'We'll let you off this once,
but don't do it again.'

Nor are the Scots ashamed of their murder buildings.

In 1561, David Rizzio, a native of Turin, went to Edinburgh
in the suite of the ambassador of Piedmont. He was a handsome fellow and also an excellent bass singer. Mary, Queen of
Scots, wanted a bass singer, and after a while Rizzio entered
her service. Quite soon he became her *valet de chambre* and
finally her private secretary for correspondence with France.
Her marriage to the young Lord Darnley, her cousin, in 1565
did nothing to undermine Rizzio's position. After a few

months, however, Darnley, who presumably could not sing a note, demanded the 'crown matrimonial' which would have made him royal, independently of the Queen. On Rizzio's advice, Mary refused. Darnley, who had been friendly with Rizzio, now professed to have discovered that he was the Queen's lover, and began to plan his murder.

On the evening of March 9, 1566, the Earls of Morton and Lindsay, at the head of a troop of their men-at-arms, burst into Mary's supper room in the Edinburgh palace of Holyrood. Rizzio was there with her; and before her eyes they dragged him out and killed him with their daggers.

There is no mystery or fascination about the murder of Rizzio. It was a shoddy piece of butchery. Yet, the Scots make no attempt to hush up the affair. They do not change the name of the Royal Palace of Holyrood or rearrange the rooms so as to confuse the murder student. They let a brass plaque into the floor at the spot where Rizzio was done to death, so that all who wish to do so may reconstruct the crime for themselves.

Unfortunately, the installation of engraved metal plaques is an expensive business; but the Scottish attitude towards murder remains as liberal as ever; even when the murderer is not of noble birth. A murder tour of Scotland is an invigorating experience.

Edinburgh, whose citizens will perhaps forgive me, has never had quite the cachet as a murder-city that Glasgow has. After all, where else but in Glasgow is it possible to find in, or within a few hundred yards of, a single city street, the locations of no less than four *classic* murder cases; cases that have been argued and re-argued by murder-tasters throughout the civilised world? However, by less exalted standards of comparison, Edinburgh is still richly endowed. The names of Burke and Hare alone would qualify it for inclusion among the top-ten murder cities of the Western world. Add to them such names as those of Lady Warriston (who killed her husband), Nicol Muschet and the Reverend Mr Kello (who killed their wives) and John Donald Merrett (who, having been acquitted on a charge of killing his mother in 1927, did kill his wife and mother-in-law in 1954) and it is evident that Edinburgh's record must be treated with respect.

It was in the year 1600 that Lady Warriston, having 'conceived one deadly rancour, hatred and malice' against her husband, the Laird, 'for the alleged biting of her in the arm and striking her divers times,' incited her servants to strangle him. They did. As a result, all except one were tried, convicted and condemned to death by being burnt. The one, Robert Weir, was not caught until four years later. He was executed by being broken on the wheel. Lady Warriston, in view of her social position, was finally beheaded instead of being burnt. Her public execution was remarkable for the vast crowds which attended it (at four o'clock in the morning) and for her sanctimonious declarations of repentance. It is tempting to assert that the house of Warriston is still there; but truth to tell the old place was rebuilt in the eighteenth century. However (trust the Scots), the whole affair was celebrated in a number of popular ballads entitled *The Laird of Warriston*, no less than three variants of which were still being sung and recited two hundred and fifty years after the commission of the crime that inspired them.

This excellent custom of commemorating famous crimes in verse has persisted in Scotland. What student of murder does not know these famous lines?

> *Up the close and doun the stair,*
> *But and ben wi' Burke and Hare.*
> *Burke's the butcher, Hare's the thief,*
> *Knox the boy that buys the beef.*

A crisp enough summary of the affair, though not as accurate as one could wish. To call Hare a thief merely in order to make a rhyme for 'beef' is mere ribaldry. The facts are more interesting.

In 1827, William Hare kept a doss-house called Log's Lodging in Tanners Close, a dark alleyway off the West Port, a slum street lying south-west of Edinburgh Castle. One of his permanent lodgers was a cobbler named William Burke. Both men had originally come from Ireland to work as labourers on the Union Canal.

In November of that year, an old army pensioner named Donald who had been lodging with Hare, died just before his quarterly pension was due. As a result, he died owing Hare a quarter's rent—four pounds.

Brooding over this bad debt and wondering how it might be recovered, Hare had an idea.

The Edinburgh medical school had long suffered from a shortage of subjects for dissection, the number of dead bodies allocated by law for the purpose having proved quite inadequate to the needs of the new department of anatomy. For a while, the students themselves had repaired these deficiencies by stealing bodies from graveyards; but gradually the practice of 'body-snatching' had been placed on a more business-like footing by professional ruffians known as Resurrection Men. The 'black market' price paid by the school for a body in good condition was anything up to ten pounds.

It was Hare's idea, then, to sell Donald's body to 'the doctors'; and because he needed someone to help him, he confided in his lodger, Burke.

Burke was willing. That night, the pair removed the body from the coffin, which had been nailed down by the parish undertaker in preparation for the funeral. Then, having weighted the coffin with timber from the tanning yard near by and re-sealed it, they set out with the body in a sack to call on Professor Munro of the anatomical school. On the way there, they stopped a young man and asked him to direct them. Learning their errand, the young man, who was a student of Professor Munro's rival, the brilliant anatomist Dr Knox, directed them to the latter's rooms at 10 Surgeon's Square. Knox's assistants were on duty that night. They naturally assumed, when Burke and Hare arrived, that they were dealing with ordinary Resurrection Men. They paid seven pounds ten shillings for Donald and added a fatal invitation. They would be glad, they said, to see Burke and Hare again when they had another body to dispose of.

To every sort of business enterprise there come, sooner or later, the clear-thinking men who break through the established order of things to achieve a new synthesis, a new rationalisation of the law of supply and demand. It was so with Burke and Hare. That night a single thought process illuminated both their minds. If you could get seven pounds ten apiece for dead bodies, why grub about, as the Resurrection Men did, stealing the things? Why not simply manufacture them?

During the next eleven months, Burke and Hare, assisted by their women, murdered no fewer than sixteen persons and sold their corpses to Dr Knox. The victims were mostly friendless down-and-outs, spotted by one or other of the quartet as suitable. The method was to offer the victim free bed and board for the night, make him (or her) dead drunk and then smother him. In the morning, they would undress the corpse, put it in a tea chest and inform Dr Knox that they had another subject. The doctor would send a porter that evening to meet them at the back of the Castle and to take delivery. As the doctor approved of the subjects being 'so fresh,' he usually paid the top price—ten pounds. He asked no questions.

In the summer of 1828, the men quarrelled over the division of the spoils, and Burke, the senior partner, went off in a huff to live in another lodging. But now they needed one another and the association was soon resumed. If they had not become careless about concealing their handiwork while it was awaiting delivery, they might have lasted longer. On the night of October 31 they murdered an old woman named Mrs Docherty, stripped off her clothes and left her body under a heap of straw in the house. A Mrs Gray, one of Burke's fellow lodgers, was curious to know what was there. When he was out of the way, she had a look. Then, she and her husband went to the police.

The game was up. Hare and Mrs Hare promptly 'turned King's Evidence' and so secured legal immunity for themselves. It was their evidence that hanged Burke. Helen M'Dougal (Burke's lady), was acquitted. Hare, however, had a worse fate than hanging in store for him. Incensed by the deal made with him by the Public Prosecutor, a Scottish crowd tried to lynch him. Escaping, with difficulty, to England, or so the story goes, he was there recognised by a crowd of workmen who threw him into a lime pit. The lime blinded him. The remainder of his life he spent in London, begging along Oxford Street.

Dr Knox was an arrogant man and his bland efforts to disclaim all responsibility for the crimes of his jackals met with small success. His professional downfall was complete. He died in London of apoplexy in 1862.

Tanners Close is still there, as dark and as squalid as ever, though Log's Lodging House was demolished in 1902. In its place stands a tenement building with a small glum-looking shop behind it. The shop belongs to a dealer in ladies' and gents' second-hand clothing.

And so to Glasgow.

The years from 1857 to 1865 were undoubtedly the Golden period of Scottish murder. In that brief space of time, and in a city area of less than a square mile, were enacted three of the most celebrated murder cases of all time; those of Madeleine Smith, Jessie M'Lachlan and Dr Pritchard. In 1908 further lustre was added to the area by the Oscar Slater case.

Sauchiehall Street is in the centre of Glasgow. Number 249 is a smart dress shop. The two floors above it are owned by the same people who own the dress shop, and are tricked out with cream and green paint and wrought-iron window boxes.

In 1865 there was no shop below. The three floors made a single private house. The number on the front door was 131* and the owner was Edward William Pritchard, the poisoner.

Dr Pritchard began his professional career as an assistant surgeon in the Royal Navy. In 1850 he married Mary Jane Taylor, the daughter of an Edinburgh merchant. In 1851, and with the financial assistance of his wife's family, he set up in private practice at Filey in Yorkshire. He did not last long there. 'He was fluent, plausible, amorous, politely impudent and singularly untruthful,' wrote a man who knew him at that time. 'His amativeness led him into some amours that did not increase the public confidence in him as a medical man; and his unveracity became so notorious that, in his attempts to deceive others, he succeeded only in deceiving himself.'

They have shrewd eyes in Yorkshire. They missed only one important aspect of his character; his capacity for cold-blooded cruelty.

He began to practise in Glasgow in 1860. Almost from the beginning his professional colleagues disliked and distrusted him, and his attempts to join the various medical societies

* I hasten to absolve Glasgow of intent to deceive. The former address was 131 Clarence Place. When Clarence Place was incorporated into Sauchiehall Street, re-numbering of the houses was unavoidable.

were unsuccessful. Blithely attributing these set-backs to professional jealousy, Dr Pritchard embarked on a personal publicity campaign. He gave lectures on the subject of his travels (on one such occasion he claimed to have 'hunted the Nubian lion in the prairies of North America'), he supplied photographs of his handsome bearded face to local shops for sale, and he cultivated the local Freemasons. After a while he succeeded in building up a fairly substantial practice, although his habit of attempting to seduce his women patients led to troublesome incidents.

One night in May, 1863, a significant event occurred. While Dr Pritchard was alone in his house with a young servant girl, the house* caught fire. As a result, the girl lost her life, and Dr Pritchard put in a big claim on the insurance company for some jewellery which he said had been destroyed. The insurance company refused to pay. Moreover, the circumstances of the girl's death were so suspicious that, after the post mortem examination, Dr Pritchard was closely questioned by the police. No further action was taken against him, however. Perhaps the fact gave him confidence. When he moved into the Sauchiehall Street house the following year, he had already seduced the dead housemaid's successor, Mary M'Leod, a girl of fifteen, and told her that he would marry her if Mrs Pritchard should die before him.

However, Pritchard's motive for murdering his wife has never been clearly established. In his three confessions he attributed his crime variously and unconvincingly to his infatuation with Mary M'Leod, to a 'species of terrible madness' and to the excessive use of 'ardent spirits'; but the habit of unveracity was too much for him; his 'confessions' are self-contradictory, and in one of them he even claimed that the housemaid Mary was an accessory to the murder of Mrs

* Not his Sauchiehall Street house; an earlier one, 11 Berkeley Terrace.

Pritchard. The probability is that he murdered his wife partly for her small income and partly because he was tired of her. She certainly knew about his affair with Mary (she had caught him with her in a bedroom) and she probably knew about his other amorous exploits, too. Moreover, he was in constant financial difficulties from which her family had on several occasions been obliged to rescue him. Mrs Pritchard cannot have been a very sympathetic helpmate at the time. There is a discernible malevolence in the method of killing her which he chose. He poisoned her, very slowly and painfully, with doses of antimony and aconite.

His murder of Mrs Taylor, his mother-in-law, is easier to explain.

Early in 1865, when he began to poison his wife, Mrs Taylor came from Edinburgh to nurse the invalid. It now seems reasonably certain that her suspicions about the true nature of the illness were aroused, and that she made the stupid mistake of telling her son-in-law about them. At all events, within two weeks of her arrival she was dead. Mrs Pritchard lived on wretchedly for a further three weeks; then she, too, died.

An anonymous letter to the authorities led to an autopsy on Mrs Pritchard, the exhumation of Mrs Taylor and the arrest of Pritchard. The writer of the letter is said to have been another doctor practising in Sauchiehall Street.

The hanging of Dr Pritchard was the last public execution to take place in Glasgow. The behaviour of the crowd was curious. Immediately after the hanging, many were observed shedding tears; and when Calcraft, the hangman, came down from the scaffold he was booed.

An incredible amount of poisoning seems to have gone on in Scotland during the earlier part of the nineteenth century. In the year 1827, for example, there were no less than three cases of murder by arsenic. In 1843 a Scottish poisoning case was even brought to the official notice of the President of the United States.

If you drive out of Glasgow to Renfrew and then two miles along the main Renfrew–Greenock road to the village of Inchinnan, you will see the 'Town of Inchinnan' Farm. The grey, harled house with its whitewashed outbuildings stands back about a hundred yards from the main road, in the middle of flat farming country. It is owned today by Matthew Gilmour.

In 1842, the owner was Mr Gilmour's great-uncle, John, and in November of that year he married a Miss Christina Cochran. She was an attractive girl, the eldest daughter of an Ayrshire farmer and apparently an excellent match for John. What he did not know about her was that she was already in love with a local youth who could not afford to marry. The marriage with John Gilmour was of her parents' devising.

It lasted about six weeks, and Christina refused to consummate it. On the day after Christmas, she told her maid to buy her some arsenic; and two days later her husband became very sick. He recovered, however, and early in January she bought some more arsenic. A few days after that her husband died. Christina returned to her parents' farm.

Rumour soon got busy. When Christina's father heard that John Gilmour's body was to be exhumed, he demonstrated his opinion of the situation by hustling her off to Liverpool and putting her on board a ship bound for New York. In June 1843 the Scottish police applied to the State of New York for her extradition on a charge of murder.

Her New York lawyer pleaded that she was insane. When a panel of doctors had decided that she was only pretending to be insane, he appealed to President Tyler. The President was unmoved, and in the end Christina was taken back to Scotland to be tried. There, however, the jury could not quite bring themselves to believe that so young and gentle a girl could poison her husband. Perhaps the fact that her father and brother had destroyed a letter from her to her lover admitting the purchase of the arsenic, made their task easier. At all events they brought in a verdict of Not Proven, and the prisoner was free.

Jessie M'Lachlan of Glasgow was not so fortunate.

17 Sandyford Place is now occupied by a medical research trust. In 1862 it was the home of John Fleming, an accountant, and his family. With them, too, lived his eighty-seven-year-old father, James Fleming. The family used to go away to their Clydeside villa for the week-ends, leaving the old man and a servant girl named M'Pherson in charge of the town house.

One Monday afternoon in July the Flemings arrived home to find the old man apparently alone. He said that the girl M'Pherson had gone away. In fact, she was lying in her basement room, hacked to death with a butcher's cleaver. When this was discovered, a doctor was immediately sent for. After some thought, he gave his opinion. 'This,' he said shrewdly, 'is certainly not suicide.' His name, happily, was Dr Watson.

On the Wednesday, old Mr Fleming was arrested. Then, Jessie M'Lachlan, a former servant of the Fleming family, was found to have pawned some silver stolen from the house, and she was arrested in his place. She stood trial for murder and was convicted. She had made the fatal mistake of trying to lie her way out of the situation in which she found herself. Only after her conviction did she tell what sounded like the truth.

The dead girl M'Pherson had been a friend of hers and, on the Friday night, Jessie had called in to sit with her and share a bottle of rum. Old Fleming had been there. After a while, the old man had sent Jessie out to get another bottle. When she returned, she found M'Pherson lying senseless with a head wound. Old Fleming said that he had not meant to hurt her.

When the girl recovered consciousness, she told Jessie that the old man had 'attempted to take liberties with her' and that when she had threatened to tell his son, he had hit her. When Jessie had said that they must call a doctor, the old man had locked the doors and said that nothing must be known of the matter. When Jessie had tried to force her way out of the house, the old man had attacked the injured girl again, hitting her with the cleaver until she died. Then, he had told Jessie that she was an accessory to the murder and that they must fake a robbery. Jessie had lost her head and agreed, taking away with her the silver and some clothing he gave her to lend colour to the robbery story.

The judge decided that this was a 'tissue of wicked falsehoods' and promptly sentenced her to death. But others were not so certain. Old Fleming had a peculiar reputation. Jessie's sentence was commuted to penal servitude.

She served fifteen years in prison and later went to America. She died at Port Huron, Michigan.

But it is Madeleine who must rate as America's most distinguished Scottish murder immigrant.

In the winter of 1856 there moved into 7 Blythswood Square, Glasgow, a family named Smith. Mr Smith was a highly respected architect. Mrs Smith was a staid, submissive Victorian wife. They had five children. Madeleine was the eldest.

In the previous year she had been introduced by a mutual acquaintance to a young Channel Islander, Pierre Emile L'Angelier, who worked as a clerk for a seed merchant. To the nineteen-year-old Madeleine he had seemed a romantic figure. He had lived in Paris and fought with the National Guard in the French revolution of 1848, or so he said. He talked of love and broken hearts and suicide and dramatic plans for emigrating to South America. He was most unlike the worthy sons of her father's friends.

In fact, he was a vain, snobbish, calculating little prig. Nothing sums him up better than his own letter to his 'Mimi' (as he called Madeleine) written the morning after he had seduced her. 'I am sad at what we did,' he wrote; 'I regret it very much. Why, Mimi, did you give way after your promises? ... I have given you warning long enough to improve yourself. Sometimes I think you take no notice of my wishes. . . .'

A few months after their first meeting, Mr Smith got to hear of the acquaintance and forbade it. Dutifully, Madeleine wrote to L'Angelier ending their correspondence. But he was not put off so easily. He had made up his mind to marry into the Smith family and so acquire the respectability and financial security he craved. He therefore enlisted the services of a sentimental elderly lady, who had befriended him, as a go-between. Soon the relationship was resumed clandestinely. The seduction was accomplished in the garden of Mr Smith's country house on the Clyde, the following year.

Now, Madeleine may have been inexperienced, but she was no ordinary Victorian miss. One thing that emerges clearly from the hundreds of letters that she wrote to L'Angelier (and which deeply shocked the court at her trial) is her frank enjoyment of the physical side of their relationship. 'For it is a pleasure, and no one can deny that. It is but human nature. Is not every one who *loves* of the same mind? Yes.' In 1856 that was an unforgivable indecency; except to Madeleine. To her, it was a simple fact, and not even the incessant preaching of her lover could change her opinion. She was a clear-sighted and determined young woman. When the family moved to Blythswood Square, she elected to sleep in the basement so that she could admit L'Angelier through the area door at night. There were bars over the windows of the room, and he used to rattle his cane against them as he passed along the pavement outside, to signal his arrival. Sometimes, it would be unsafe for him to come in. Then, she would pass a letter to him through the bars and they would talk softly. At other times, when the rest of the family were sound asleep and the coast was clear, he would be admitted and she would make cocoa for him in the kitchen.

By the end of 1856, however, both were getting tired of this arrangement; he, because he wanted to be accepted openly by her family and enter by the front door; she, because she was tired of his preaching and fault-finding, and because her common-sense now told her that there was no future in their relationship. At one point she had offered to leave her family, marry him and live on his clerk's wages if he were willing. When he had refused, that had been the end for her. She had at last seen through him. There were quarrels. In January, 1857, she became engaged to a friend of her father's, a Glasgow merchant named Minnoch.

L'Angelier's reaction to her cool note informing him that the affair was at an end and requesting him to return her letters and portrait, was terrifying. Yes, he would return her letters, but to her father, who should now know of everything that had passed between them, and that she was, in effect, already Mrs L'Angelier. Madeleine wrote back frantically begging for mercy. 'Do nothing 'til I see you,' her letter ends: 'for the love of heaven do nothing.'

L'Angelier relented after a few days, but only on condition that their relationship was resumed, and on the understanding that she was not in fact engaged to Minnoch. She had gained a little time. The reconciliation took place on February 12. During that week, she tried unsuccessfully to buy prussic acid. On the 21st, she succeeded in buying arsenic, 'to kill rats.' Twenty-four hours later, L'Angelier drank cocoa she made for him and was very ill. He recovered. On March 21 she wrote to him: 'Come to me, sweet one. I waited and waited for you, but you came not. I shall wait again tomorrow night, same hour and arrangement. Do come, sweet love, my own dear love of a sweetheart.'

He obeyed the summons. In the early hours of the morning of the 23rd, he staggered back to the door of his lodging, so doubled up with pain that he was unable to use the door key. His landlady let him in and sent for a doctor. Later that day, he died.

When Madeleine was arrested, Mr and Mrs Smith took to their bed and stayed in it until after the trial. Authority respected their feelings; even spared them the ordeal of giving evidence. However, Madeleine had no need of their moral support. In spite of the revelations about her private life and in spite of the great danger that she was in, she remained completely calm and self-assured throughout the nine days of her trial. Even the verdict of Not Proven produced from her no more than a faint smile, though in a letter she wrote a few days later, she expressed herself as pleased with the loud cheers that greeted the announcement of it.

The house in Blythswood Square is safely preserved by the authorities of the Agricultural College which now occupies it, and the adjacent property. Even Madeleine's basement room, that famous room with its barred windows, is still intact. It is now one of the college staff lavatories.

And Madeleine herself?

Four years after the trial, she married George Wardle, a London artist and an associate of William Morris. She had three children, became a Socialist, started the fashion of using mats on the dinner table instead of a tablecloth, and numbered among her acquaintances the young G. B. Shaw. When her husband died she lived for a time in Staffordshire and then emigrated to America, where she met a Mr Sheehy and lived with him until he died in 1926. When she was ninety, a

Hollywood film company found her and tried to persuade her to appear in a film about her own story. She refused and was threatened with deportation as an undesirable alien. But she fought back and won. She always had. She died in 1928, and was buried under the name of Lena Wardle Sheehy in Mount Hope Cemetery, New York.

She was a remarkable woman. Perhaps the Society would consider putting some flowers on her grave. I am sure that Scotland would appreciate the gesture.

3

France

Gentlemen, I have received a number of private requests from members for information about the current murder situation in France.

Several of these requests have been made almost furtively; others in such equivocal terms that I have only been able to guess at their real meaning. However, all of them seemed to be based on a common attitude. As one member remarked with a leer: 'Put the words "France" and "murder" side by side, breathe on them gently and—*click*—you have *crime passionel.* Right?'

Others were even more enthusiastic. France, they assured me, is the country in which the heart rules the head, where the feelings of the deceived husband or the discarded mistress are fully understood by toddlers of both sexes long before they learn to read, where love conquers all. Nowhere else, they said, have juries so much sympathy for the unhappy killer; nowhere else is justice so benevolent. And was there not a famous criminal lawyer who said that, if he had committed murder and hoped to get away with it, he would sooner be tried by a French court than any other in the world? Almost certainly there was. France is the one place where the murderer is understood and appreciated. *Vive le crime passionel!*

I feel it necessary to warn any of you gentlemen who may be thinking of basing a family excursion to France on those assumptions, that the facts are different. Under the circumstances, too, I thought it as well to advise your Honorary Secretary that, much as I enjoy the company of female murder-tasters, it would, in my opinion, be prudent in this case to neglect to notify the female membership of the Society of the time and place of this little talk.

Attempts are always being made to ascribe to the murders of this country or that a distinct national flavour. The characteristic American murder, for instance, has been held to be the open air shooting; those murderers who cut their victims up, put the pieces in trunks and deposit them in the cloakrooms of main line railway termini are attributed mainly to England; the nineteenth century Scottish poisoners, it is said, form as clearly differentiated a group as the Renaissance Italians.

However, there is one fact about murder in France of which we can be absolutely certain. If there is such a thing as a characteristically French murder, it is not the *crime passionel*. Even in the thirties, the number of murders which came into that category was a bare twelve per cent of the total. And, gentlemen, take note of this; with a few pathetic exceptions, the only French killers who have ever successfully used the conception of the *crime passionel* as a defence have been women. Where a woman is concerned, indeed, a *crime passionel* does not have to be committed in a moment of sudden overwhelming emotion. It can be premeditated.

The case of Henriette Caillaux (1914) is a famous example.

She was the second wife of Joseph Caillaux, the French Minister of Finance, and their relationship had been a stormy one. As Mademoiselle 'Riri' Rainouard, she had been the Minister's mistress, until in 1909 an unfortunate incident occurred. In a period of special ardour the Minister had written his Riri some letters. Interspersed with his protestations of love ('A thousand million kisses on every part of your adorable little body') had been some candid explanations of his current political manœuvrings. When, on reflection, the Minister had decided that he had been indiscreet, he had asked her to send the letters back.

Riri had done so. However, the Minister's mood of discretion had passed. Instead of destroying the letters, he had merely locked them in a drawer. The first Madame Caillaux, a watchful woman, had thereupon procured a duplicate key and taken possession.

For a time, she used the letters to blackmail him into giving up Riri, but, after a while, she seemed to relent, and in 1911 agreed (on her terms) to a divorce. However, the divorce contract stipulated that the letters were to be destroyed, and Madame formally assured the Minister that she had carried out that part of the bargain. In October, he married Riri.

For a while they were blissfully happy. Then, the Minister learned to his horror that the letters he had believed destroyed were being offered clandestinely to his political enemies. The couple waited wretchedly for the worst.

In 1914 it came. Gaston Calmette, director of *Le Figaro*, and the most influential French journalist of the day, began in January of that year a series of violent attacks upon the Finance Minister.

French political commentators have never been mealy-mouthed, but the virulence and ferocity of Calmette's campaign was exceptional, even for those days. It is possible that he was driven by some other, more personal reason than the high-minded motives of public interest which he professed. We do not know. It no longer matters. The attacks went on, day after day, relentlessly. In March, he began to include extracts from those disastrous letters.

For a while the Minister and Riri squirmed helplessly. Then, as Calmette persisted, they became desperate. They were advised to take legal advice. The judge whom they consulted told them that there was nothing to be done in law. Incensed by this confirmation of his impotence, the Minister shouted that he would break Calmette's neck.

'When?' inquired Riri.

'Never you mind,' replied the Minister darkly.

Possibly, Riri was not satisfied with this reply. Possibly, knowing that her husband was a busy man, she wished to save him trouble. The following day she went to a gunsmith's, selected a revolver and tried it out in the company's private range. She then went home again, changed her dress and drove to the *Figaro* office.

She had to wait to see Calmette, but she got in at last.

'No doubt you are surprised to see me,' she said as he rose to greet her.

This was an understatement, but he bowed politely. 'Not at all, Madame. Please sit down.'

Instead of accepting his invitation she drew the revolver, thumbed over the safety catch and fired all six chambers at him. Four of the bullets wounded him, one of them fatally.

Riri remained calm. To those who rushed into the office and disarmed her, she said loftily: 'I am a lady. My car is waiting to take me to the police station.'

She remained calm—and ladylike—throughout her trial; and secured a complete acquittal.

Compare this with the case of the hapless Jean-Louis Verger, a mad priest, who stabbed the Archbishop of Paris to death during a service in the church of St Etienne du Mont.

Asked why he had committed the crime, he replied: 'Because I do not believe in the Immaculate Conception.'

A ten-minute examination by a court physician was sufficient to dispose of the defence's timid suggestion that Verger was insane, and to establish that he had a 'most perverse and dangerous nature.' After that, the jury had no difficulty in deciding that this was a matter for the guillotine.

More fortunate was Marcel Hilaire, the millionaire miller, who was tried in 1953 for murdering his young mistress. His lawyer's contention that it was a *crime passionel* succeeded. Instead of being guillotined, Hilaire was sentenced to life imprisonment with hard labour.

The French belief that, when murder has been done, there may sometimes be extenuating circumstances, should not be misunderstood. The patient Anglo-Saxon crowd waiting quietly outside the courthouse for a glimpse of the accused has no counterpart in France. There they make hostile demonstrations and may even try to lynch the wretch. Inside the court the same attitude prevails. Words like 'monster' and 'vile assassin' may be hurled by judge and prosecuting counsel at the accused.

Most premeditated murders are done not for passion but for profit. For the French, always hypersensitive where money matters are concerned, this makes the offence particularly disgusting. The Americans and British respond to this sort of murder with interest and requests for more details; the French respond with indignation and demands for the killer's head.

They have had plenty to be indignant about. No other country has produced so many really business-like, profit-seeking *multiple* murderers.

Early in 1918, the mayor of the small town of Gambais, just outside Paris, received a letter that puzzled him. It was from a Madame Pelat, and she wanted to know if the mayor knew of the whereabouts of her sister, Madame Collomb, who had been living with a Monsieur Cuchet at the Villa Ermitage. It puzzled him because he had, not long before, received a similar letter from the sister of a Madame Buisson who had been living at the Villa Ermitage with a Monsieur Fremyet. On looking into the matter, the mayor found not only that the registered occupier of the villa was a Monsieur Dupont, but that Dupont, Fremyet and Cuchet had all disappeared. The mayor suggested that the families of the two missing women might find it useful to compare notes. They did so. It did not take them long to conclude that Cuchet, Fremyet and Dupont were one and the same person. They informed the police.

Inspector Adam of the Criminal Investigation Department at Mantes was immediately interested. Other and similar cases of women disappearing had been reported. In the spring of 1919 a warrant was issued for the arrest of Fremyet. By one of those outrageous coincidences which make the career of the professional murderer such a heart-breaking business, Madame Buisson's sister, while out walking in Paris, happened to spot a man in the rue de Rivoli whom she recognised as the missing woman's fiancé. He was with an attractive girl. She followed the pair to a china shop and then informed the police. On being arrested, the man described himself as Lucien Guillet, engineer and mill-owner from Rocroi. His true identity was very soon established. His criminal record went back to 1900, since when he had served five prison terms for swindling. His name was Henri Désiré Landru.

When told that he was being held for murder, Landru made two remarks. 'It is a terrible thing to charge one with murder, Monsieur le Commissaire—it means a man's head.' And then he added: 'I will speak only in the presence of a lawyer.'

The first was undoubtedly prophetic, but it was the second that the police had most cause to remember. Landru's skill as an obstructionist of the law must be unique.

It is generally conceded that he murdered eleven persons in all—ten women, and the eighteen-year-old son of one of them. The pattern of the crimes was consistent and by no means original. He would insert an advertisement in a daily paper:

'*Widower with two children, aged forty-three with comfortable income, affectionate, serious and moving in good society, desires to meet widow with a view to matrimony.*' Then, he would sort the replies, choose his victim and set to work. After a brief wooing, during which he would gain control of the victim's money and possessions, he would take her for a holiday to the Villa Ermitage. Then, he would murder her, dispose of the body and return to Paris.

Yet, it took over two years from the date of his arrest to bring him to trial.

In France, the task of preparing a case for trial is in the hands of an examining magistrate, who has powers to examine witnesses, including the accused, bring about confrontations and cross-examine everyone to his heart's content. The psychological pressure on the accused of such examinations, which can (and in Landru's case did) go on for months, may be imagined. Yet Landru blandly refused to talk.

The law had one very important piece of evidence. This was a notebook found in Landru's pocket when he was arrested. It should have been damning. It was nothing less than a profit and loss account of the murders, with names, expenses and receipts from the sales of property all meticulously recorded. From an analysis of the expenses, it was even possible to note that when he had taken a woman to Gambais to murder her, he bought a return railway ticket for himself, but only a single for the victim. But Landru was not disconcerted. Pressed for explanations of the facts disclosed by the book, he took refuge in an attitude of affronted dignity. 'Monsieur le Juge,' he would repeat huffily as the interminable questionings went on, 'I will not reply to questions which are of a private nature.'

This steadfast assumption that, in pursuing their inquiries into the fates of the missing women, the examining magistrates were committing an unwarrantable and tasteless invasion of

5—A.T.K.

his privacy, was the basis of his defence; and the fact that the police were unable to produce even one of the victims' bodies made it peculiarly effective. It was alleged that he had burnt most of them in the furnace at Villa Ermitage, but the pathologists were only able to produce a number of small calcined bone fragments of dubious origin to support the allegation. Landru shrugged and said that the fragments had belonged to rabbits. Later, however, he was obliged to shore up his defences. He did this in a characteristic way. He became a man of honour who could not reveal the missing women's secrets; a suggestion hovered in the air that they had asked him to arrange their transportation to the *maisons de rendezvous* of South America. In the early days of his trial he was sardonic, even jaunty. Of his refusal to answer questions he said: 'It is not my business to help the police. Have they not been accusing me for years of deeds with which the women who disappeared never for one moment reproached me?'

But as the trial wore on, the jauntiness went. 'These charges do not frighten me. I refuse to reply to you. This matter belongs to my private life. That is no affair of the police or of the Courts of Justice.'

'Will you say nothing to save your head?' demanded the Advocate-General.

'No,' said Landru sullenly.

He kept his word. Early one cold morning a few months later he was hurried from the prison at Versailles into the Place des Tribunaux outside, and guillotined.

Nineteen twenty-one was a good year for French murder. But for the carelessness of a prison official at Fresnes, it would have been a great year.

Admittedly, Henri Girard only succeeded in committing two murders; but that was not for want of zeal. The fault lay in his method.

Moralists will enjoy this story. It was his sex-life that was at the root of the trouble. Some men accumulate housing property or stocks and shares, others collect pictures or old motor cars. Girard went in for mistresses; and not just one at a time, but two or three, each in a separate establishment of her own. Moreover, he preferred to maintain in each the belief that she was the sole object of his affections. To the tradition-ally heavy expenses of that particular hobby, there must have been added a considerable item for taxi fares. Even if, with so many other calls upon his time, he had been able to apply him-self effectively to his business as an insurance agent, his in-come would still have been inadequate. He was obliged to supplement it.

For a time, he swindled his family, but when that source at last dried up, he took to banking. His first venture, the *Crédit Général de France*, was unsuccessful. All he collected out of that was a fine and a suspended sentence of twelve months' imprison-ment. From then on, he said he was a bookmaker. In fact, he be-came a kind of confidence man, manipulating forged notes-of-hand and the like, and moved in that strange underworld which in France is called *le milieu*, but which in other countries has harsher names. For a man of his fastidious tastes it was no kind of life. He looked about for some other way of making money.

The great idea came to him at last; as it has come to so very many others. Why not insure someone's life, kill him and collect?

Girard was not foolhardy. He had been an insurance agent. He knew the ropes. The deaths had to appear natural. Very well! If they had to appear natural, why not *make* them natural. In the house of one of his mistresses in Neuilly, he set up a laboratory and began to study pathology. Later, from a firm which supplied medical schools with such materials, he bough a number of bacteria cultures.

For his first victim he chose a friendly numbskull named Louis Pernotte, who had been one of his innocent partners in the banking venture. Having insured Pernotte's life substantially with two companies, Girard set to work. A little while later the victim contracted typhoid. However, this did not prove fatal. Soon he began to get well again. Girard did some more experiments in his laboratory and then took to visiting the convalescent. On one of these visits he offered to save Madame Pernotte the trouble of giving her husband an injection prescribed by the local doctor. As she was not very good at using the hypodermic syringe, she accepted. The doctor attributed the death to complications following on typhoid. In a way, he was right.

A few months later, Girard tried the typhoid again on a man named Delmas. He recovered completely, however, and Girard began to get discouraged. But not for long. His enthusiasm for bacteriology may have waned, but he had a fresh interest to replace it—poisonous fungi.

The variety which took his fancy was that of *Amanita phalloides* and the chosen subject this time was another friend, Duroux. Having insured him in the usual way, Girard invited him to dinner and tried out the new method. It was a failure. Duroux was not even sick. Girard now prepared a stronger brew in liquid form and a day or so later continued to spike his friend's drinks with it. What followed is no tribute to his skill. *Amanita phalloides* is a deadly poison and, even today, the chances of recovery are not much better than fifty per cent. All that happened to Duroux was that he had an attack of gastric trouble.

And he came back for more. When he was well again he had another drink with Girard, and the same thing happened; and again he recovered. Girard did not bother with this unsatisfactory subject any more.

Instead, his attentions moved on to the friend of one of his mistresses, a Madame Monin. With her the stuff worked properly. He had taken out four policies on her life with four different companies. All except one paid up. The fourth asked questions and then started an inquiry.

That was the end of Girard. While he was in prison, one of his mistresses succeeded in smuggling in a culture from his laboratory. The hours he had spent there were not after all to be wasted. He died (of 'natural causes') before he came up for trial.

The greatest amateur laboratory worker of them all, however, was undoubtedly Jean-Baptiste Troppmann. Beside him, Girard was a bungler. Troppmann was only twenty-one when he was executed in 1870; yet in that short life he had not only devised a means of making prussic acid in the home, but murdered an entire family of eight persons—for money, of course. At his trial, a professor of chemistry called as a witness said of Troppmann's distillation apparatus: 'I am astonished that a man ignorant in chemistry could think out such an ingenious, intelligent method.'

Troppmann was the youngest child of a large family. The father, who ran a small engineering business at Cernay in Alsace, was a clever mechanic but a poor business man. Most of his life had been spent in fending off bankruptcy and nursing the gloomy conviction that he was the victim of plots hatched by his competitors. In her youngest child, her little Jean-Baptiste, his wife found consolation. He became her favourite, her confidant, her hope for the future.

He grew up an undersized, sickly, sour little boy, liable to sudden rages of terrifying violence. He soon compensated for his poor physique by an obsessional preoccupation with muscle-building. At school, and later as an apprentice in his father's workshop, he was loathed and feared. By the time he was fifteen he was already hard at work in his home laboratory, on the extraction of morphia from poppies. He was looking for a means with which to conquer the world of high finance. When morphia extraction proved too difficult, he turned to prussic acid.

At nineteen he was sent to assist in the erection of a machine supplied by his father to a factory in Roubaix in north-east France. It was there that he met the Kinck family.

Jean Kinck had come from Alsace, too. In Roubaix, he had built up a prosperous brush-making business and married a local girl. They had six children, the eldest of whom was fifteen. Now, homesick for Alsace, he made a friend of the young Jean-Baptiste whose cleverness he, a stupid man apart from his skill in brush-making, so much admired.

What Jean-Baptiste saw was a small fortune in the hands of eight beings less worthy than he. He decided, as a first step on his road to the summit of power, to liquidate the entire Kinck family and take over their assets.

The mechanics of the trick by means of which he induced Jean Kinck to take a trip to Alsace are unimportant. Kinck was murdered (prussic acid) near a place called Bollwiller. Then, Jean-Baptiste went to Paris. From there he sent a series of forged letters in Kinck's name to Madame Kinck, telling her of a big deal he was consummating and urging her to bring the family and all Kinck's legal papers (birth certificates, title deeds and so on) at once. He followed the letters with telegrams. Madame Kinck, who could not read and had to ask a neighbour to do so for her, finally obeyed orders. Gustave, the eldest boy, was sent first; and killed. Madame and the other children followed. Jean-Baptiste met them at the station, took them to a quiet place in the suburbs and butchered the lot. He used no prussic acid now—just a spade, a knife, an axe and his bare hands.

Perhaps he became tired; perhaps he was careless. He did not bury them deeply enough. The following day a farm labourer found them; and a few days after that the police found Jean-Baptiste.

The defence said he was not sane; but, as we have seen, pleas of insanity in murder cases have never been very successful in France.

Eugene Weidmann, tried in 1939 for the murder of six persons, had no better luck. A hopeless schizophrenic, he had been in and out of prison and psychiatrists' offices since he was fourteen. Yet the prosecution showed that he had murdered for profit and the die was cast. Useless to argue that the profits were paltry and their significance merely symbolic. Profits there had been and that was enough. 'Must justice always be a slaughter house?' demanded Weidmann's lawyer in his speech for the defence. A Versailles jury replied in the affirmative. A large crowd collected to whistle and boo as the condemned man was led to his execution.

Frankly, Weidmann only just escapes amateur status. What, it may be asked, has France to offer that can compare with the phenomena of Murder, Inc., in America or of John George Haigh in Britain?

The answer is Marcel-André-Henri-Felix Petiot, the greatest business man of them all.

His fabulous career began when he was sixteen; and it began typically. He was caught pilfering from letter boxes.

That was just before the first World War. He was an orphan in the care of a respectable woman, an aunt who was his legal guardian, and not too much was made of the letter box affair. When he left school he studied medicine until, in 1916, he was conscripted into the army.

His next criminal venture was more profitable. He peddled narcotic drugs stolen from casualty clearing stations in the field. When the army finally caught him, they decided that he was a shell-shock case (he had earlier been wounded in the foot) and gave him an honourable discharge on medical grounds. He was a good-looking, friendly, likeable fellow.

On leaving the army he resumed his medical studies and, after a period as a student in an insane asylum, was awarded his doctorate. In 1921, he set up practice in Villeneuve-sur-Yonne.

He was immediately successful; at least in building up the practice. Later came periods of difficulty and embarrassment. Quite early in his career, for example, an attractive girl whom he had employed as a housekeeper became pregnant and disappeared. She was never heard of again. And then in 1930, a woman who managed a local store was murdered by someone who removed a substantial sum of money from the till. An imprudent gossip, who suggested that Dr Petiot might have been concerned, also died. Dr Petiot had been treating this person for rheumatism at the time; but Dr Petiot, who also conducted the autopsy, was able to reassure the townsfolk; the man had died from natural causes.

The doctor was in a strong position by then, though. He had been elected Councillor and was now Mayor of the district, a married man with a family, respected by all. The slanders of his political opponents were beneath contempt.

In 1932, however, he made an error of judgment. There had been a number of thefts of municipal property. The police set a watch. Mayor Petiot was caught in the act of stealing and sentenced to three months' imprisonment. Upon his release, he moved his practice to Paris.

We next hear of him there in 1936, when he was arrested for shop-lifting. The good looks and the charm worked yet again. The court advised him to seek psychiatric treatment. He went back to his practice.

The war of 1939 came. The doctor remained in Paris during the German occupation, and 1942 found him up to his old tricks. He was charged with peddling narcotics; but the charges never came to anything. The witnesses just disappeared; usually after a consultation with the doctor. By now, he had more serious matters on his mind.

In 1941 he had acquired a house in the rue Lesueur, a fashionable street near the Etoile, and he had commissioned a firm of builders to carry out certain alterations. Their major task was to construct a windowless and sound-proof room, in which, he said, he wished to carry out scientific experiments involving electrical apparatus which might cause annoyance to the neighbours. A small glass-covered peep-hole was to be let into the wall of the room.

At the same time, the doctor had let it be known in the right quarters that those who, because of their race or political opinions, wished to leave conquered France for Spain or Britain or America might do worse than consult Dr Petiot.

Then he sat back and waited for business.

It came. The mechanism was apparently quite simple. At the first interview the would-be traveller was given his orders. He was to report at such and such a time, with a minimum of baggage and any valuables he wanted to take with him plus a fee of two thousand American dollars. He must tell no one where he was going or when. At the second interview, the fee was collected and traveller ushered to the 'secret exit.' This was the sound-proof room.

There are two theories about the method Dr Petiot used to kill his victims. One says that he 'inoculated' them for the journey. The other maintains that he gassed them in the room. Nobody who got as far as the room ever returned to tell us. The doctor was very efficient; so efficient, that he was even arrested by the Gestapo for aiding the escape of disaffected persons, and held for a time on suspicion.

It was not until March, 1944, that things went really wrong for him.

The doctor's next-door neighbour in the rue Lesueur complained to the police of a bad smell coming from a chimney in the doctor's house. The chimney appeared to be on fire. The police investigated and sent for the fire brigade. They also summoned Dr Petiot from a house near by. By the time he arrived, the fire brigade had broken in and found a corpse burning in the furnace. They had also found the remains of twenty-six other men and women in the cellars.

The doctor was equal to the situation. Drawing the senior police officer aside, he explained impatiently that the house was used by the resistance movement as a place of execution. By blundering in like that the police had risked the lives of countless patriots. Furtively and apologetically, the police withdrew. It was some hours before they had second thoughts on the subject. By then the doctor had left for the country.

It took six months for the police to catch up with him. At his trial, he claimed that the total number of his victims was sixty-three, but said that they were all Germans or collaborators. There was no reason to question his arithmetic; but the charm had worn thin and nobody believed the rest of his story.

The French psychiatrists who examined him found no signs of insanity. His trouble, they said, was that he was 'morally retarded.'

Unmoved, the French public expressed their disapproval in the usual manner. In May, 1946, he was guillotined.

4

Criminal London

Ladies and gentlemen, it was with deep emotion that I learned of your Society's plan to make a pilgrimage to London during the forthcoming year. I well know how much hope and encouragement the news will bring to British murder-tasters in their struggle to preserve the murder-homes of England. If, as your President has so flatteringly suggested, these talks of mine have in some measure contributed to the project, then I am proud as well as happy.

I know, of course, that some members have expressed concern as to the possible effects of the pilgrimage on Anglo-American relations; but let me reassure them.

Naturally, inevitably, there will be newspaper headlines—'American Ghouls to Honour Christie,' 'Disgraceful Scenes in Hilldrop Crescent,' and so on—but there will be no real unfriendliness. As long as members are aware of certain truths, certain contradictions, both sides will have a thoroughly good time.

There is nothing that the Londoner relishes more than a good crime, unless it is the moral indignation that goes with his enjoyment of it. Nor is this a recent enthusiasm, the result, as some censorious persons claim, of the corrupting influence of prurient newspapers and magazines.

Allow me to read to you a passage from a book about London.

'Who would imagine that in a Kingdom so fertile in all sorts of wholesome discipline, there should grow up such ranck and such pestilent beds of hemlock; that in the very hart of a state so rarely governed and dieted by good lawes, there should breede such loathsome and such ulcerous impostumes? that in a City so politick, so civill, and so severe, such ugly, base, and bold impieties dare shew their faces? What an Army of insufferable *Abuses*, detestable *Vices*, most damnable *Villanies*, abominable *Pollutions*, inexplicable *Mischiefes*, sordid *Inquinations*, *horrible* and *Hel-hound-like perpetrated* flagitious enormities have beene here ministered together?'

That is from *The Belman of London* by Thomas Dekker, published in 1608. The title page of the first edition announced, with a smack of the lips, that it was 'Bringing to light the most notorious villanies that are now practised in the Kingdome,' and recommended it as, 'Profitable for Gentlemen, Lawyers, Merchants, Citizens, Farmers, Masters of Households, and all sorts of servants, to marke, and *delightful for all men to Reade*.'* In the golden age of reason the massive voice of Doctor Samuel Johnson was raised to challenge a decision of the Sheriffs of Newgate to conduct their hangings at the prison. 'Sir,' he groused to Boswell, 'executions are intended to draw spectators. If they do not draw spectators, they do not answer their purpose. The old method was most satisfactory to all parties; the public were gratified by a procession, the criminal was supported by it. Why is all this to be swept away?'

What the doctor was complaining about, be it noted, was not that the executions were to be private (over eighty years were to go by before hangings ceased to be a public entertainment in London), but that the old custom of parading the condemned person and the hangman in a cart through the streets

* The original publisher's italics.

to Tyburn gallows, was to be abolished.* And there is no
doubt that he was voicing popular feeling on the subject.
Twenty thousand people would turn out to see an important
hanging; and, as, at the time, there were some two hundred
offences that carried the death penalty, Londoners had plenty
of hangings from which to choose. Since 1868 there have been
no public executions in London (Michael Barrett, the Fenian,
was the subject of the last) and today only four capital charges
remain—high treason, murder, piracy with violence and (for
some obscure reason) the 'destruction of dockyards.' Small
wonder that the Londoner counts on his Sunday newspaper
to make the most of what is left, and that when fact began to
fail him, he should turn so readily to fiction. The detective
story may have been born in the mind of Edgar Allan Poe,
but it was London that fed it, clothed it and brought it to
maturity.

Members might suppose, then, that, faced by the inquiring
visitor anxious to savour Criminal London at its seamiest, the
proud, eager Londoner would be ready with a list of all the
liveliest sinks of iniquity, a warning against con-men, and
directions for getting to the site of the latest razor-slashing
incident before the blood is cleaned up. But no. What the
unfortunate visitor is most likely to get is a smug, cliché-
packed lecture about how law-abiding London is, how polite
and gentlemanly the police are, how they don't carry guns,
how even the few petty crooks there are (and what big city
doesn't have at least a few?) always respect the copper on the
beat, how Scotland Yard always gets its man, and how, if you
leave your wallet in a London taxi, all you have to do to get it

* The Sheriffs were moved by no humanitarian considerations. They wanted
the executions right outside the prison so that the prisoners might 'derive a useful lesson of duty and obedience and a strong admonition to repentance from the
presence of the heavy hand of justice so near the walls.'

back is go to the Lost Property Office, because Londoners are so honest. As Americans you may even have to endure a statistical bromide, too; Chicago had 326 murders in 1948, whereas London with over double the population had only 31 murders during the same period.

All this is not mere hypocrisy. There is a criminal and a policeman inside every human being; and in the breast of the law-abiding Londoner the war between the two is waged with particular ferocity. But it is waged in silence, and the official communiqués always tell of victories for the policemen. It is only in the turbulent back-streets of the London mind that the ghosts of priggers and whip-jacks, of draw-latches, fraters and Abraham men, are still allowed to roister with their doxies through the stews and trugging shops of Thomas Dekker's city. There no policeman walks his beat. The bell of Newgate Prison has been silent now for over fifty years; but its echoes have not ceased, and, in the blood flowing so sedately through the modern Londoner's veins, there is still something that quickens to that far-off sound. It is an old, cruel lust, and he prefers to refer to it deprecatingly as a taste for the macabre.

Newgate! For many a Londoner the very word is still a part of childhood. 'Go and wash your face,' his mother used to tell him. 'You're as black as Newgate's knocker!' Nothing, he knew, could ever be blacker.

Newgate was built on to the old city wall as an additional defence work in the twelfth century. In those days city gate fortifications were often used as prisons, and the New gate was exceptional only in that it remained a prison for over seven centuries, 'the repository,' says its historian, 'of more human suffering and more human sorrow than any other building in the City of London.' In the fifteenth century, a Lord Mayor of London named Whittington tried to ease the lot of the prisoners; and when he died, his money, bequeathed to charity, was used to rebuild the prison. It was from Dick Whittington's Newgate, with its stone figure of a cat at the feet of Liberty, that Dick Turpin, Jack Sheppard and Claude Duval went to the gallows. In the eighteenth century it was again rebuilt. But it was already a legend and no amount of rebuilding could change its evil reputation. Newgate was Newgate, and Londoners were soon reminded of the fact when 'gaol fever' (typhoid) from the new prison killed off several judges who held court in the adjacent Sessions House. In 1827, after a visit to London, Heine, the German poet, wrote that the very name of Newgate filled the mind with horror.

Yet for the Londoner there was pride and awe as well in his feelings about the place. When Wandsworth Prison was built, critics of its architecture complained that it lacked the 'fine, gloomy solemnity of Newgate,' and it was not until 1902 that Newgate itself was finally demolished. All that is left of it now is the water conduit which some charitable grocer installed in the fifteenth century so that the prisoners should not die of thirst. In the old building's place stands the Central Criminal Court, commonly known by the name of the lane that runs between Newgate Street and Ludgate Hill—the Old Bailey.

The shade of Newgate was certainly hovering at the architect's elbow when he designed it. The 'fine, gloomy solemnity' of the Old Bailey is in every sense worthy of the site it occupies. Its appearance produces immediate feelings of depression and guilt. Many remarkable murderers have been tried there. After a few minutes of the echoing gloom within, one wonders why they troubled to defend themselves. The Old Bailey is the place of which the criminals of London have always been most afraid.

Recently, a crime reporter made a list of the types of criminal currently working in London and graded them in the order of their professional standing. Dekker listed 'roagues and vagabonds' in a similar way, using the old London thieves' cant. On the blackboard here, you may see the two lists side by side.

1608	TODAY
Barnards, *Cheators*, *Bankers* and *Gripes* (Crooked gamblers)	Confidence men
	Receivers
Charmes and *Courbers* (Burglars)	Forgers
Priggers (Horse thieves)	Mayfair cat-burglars
Whip-jackes and *Batfowlers* (Shop-lifters and smash-and-grab operators)	Big time burglars
	Safe-breakers
	Warehouse thieves
High-lawyers (Highwaymen)	Smash-and-grab men
Figgers (Pickpockets)	Pickpockets
Rufflers, *Upright-men*, *Abraham men* and *Hookers* (Hoodlums and strong-arm men)	Drug-pedlars
	Long-firm fraudsmen
Palliards and *Clapperdugeons* (Professional beggars)	Suburban burglars
	Car thieves
Fraters (Bogus charity collectors)	Sneak thieves
Dumerars (Bogus accident artists)	Crooked gamblers
Kinchin Coes (Child thieves)	Bag-snatchers
Kinchin Morts (Infant decoys hired by professional beggars)	Dog thieves
	Pimps
	Blackmailers

The first thing to be noted is the remarkable way in which the burglars have maintained their status in the face of three centuries of competition. Equally remarkable is the fall taken by the gamblers. Did they become careless? Or did the cleverer ones emigrate and go West? In 1862, the only crooked 'gamblers' listed by Mayhew in his great survey of the London underworld were three-card tricksters and pea-and-thimble men.

With the advent of the railway, horse thieves and highwaymen would obviously go out of business. A more interesting change is in the position of the con-man. In Dekker's time he seems scarcely to have existed. There are allusions in *The Belman* to 'fooletaking,' mock auctions and other 'knaverie,' but that is about all. He was certainly very low in the underworld social scale. Receivers of stolen property were not in it at all. Dekker referred to them casually as 'certaine Brokers, who traffick onely in this kind of (stolen) Merchandize and by bils of sale . . . get the goods of honest Citizens.' He did add, however, that they always made more money than the crooks who did the actual stealing. They still do, of course.

Blackmail, though again an unclassified crime, he discussed at some length. He called it 'sacking' and seems to have had a sneaking regard for its practitioners. One type of shake-down which he describes has a familiar modern ring. A gentleman finds himself in a lady's bedroom, when 'in comes a Ruffian with a drawne rapier, calles the Punck (as she is) damned whore, asks what Rogue that is, and what he does with his wife. The conclusion of all this counterfeit swaggering being a plot betwixt this panderly ruffian and the whore to geld the silly foole of all the money hee hath in his purse, and sometimes to make him (rather than his credit should be called into question) to seale a bill or bond for other sums of money at such and such daies, and so send him packing, when he hath paide too deare for a bad dish of meate which he never tasted.'

It seems odd that in today's scale of values the blackmailer rates so low. In London, he (or she) is the only criminal that other criminals get high-minded and stuffy about.

Drug-peddling carries no stigma, and, indeed, is more acceptable socially than burgling in the suburbs; but blackmail, no. Even dog-stealing (and the British are a nation of dog lovers) is preferable!

The outstanding omission from the seventeenth-century list is certainly the pimp. The reason for this seems to be Dekker's assumption that all crooks were panders anyway. True, he did single out those who lived on the immoral earnings of their innocent wives; but only to make a moral judgment. 'Infamous earthy minded *Creatures* in the Shapes of *Snailes*,' he called them. On the bawds, doxies, dells, morts and bawdy-baskets who ministered so generously to their applesquires and fancy men, he wasted no tears. 'The companion of a theefe,' he wrote, 'is commonly a *Whore*. It is not amisse, therefore, to pinion them together.'

For the sake of convenience, we had better do the same thing; not only because in London, as in most other cities, prostitution and crime are generally close relatives, but because the visitor can so easily find this gateway to the underworld for himself. He will, however, soon recognise sharp regional differences.

In Mayfair, the crooks are, on the whole, of the genteel, non-violent variety and the girls endeavour to look and behave as much like actresses as possible. Some of them even succeed. It is only when the competition tries to move in that the façade collapses and nature, red in lip and claw, re-asserts herself. Almost invariably the competition comes from the shoddy square mile of London commonly known as Soho.

The northern part of it was a nineteenth-century development. There, the streets are wider, quieter and straighter than those south of Oxford Street. In and around Warren Street cluster dozens of second-hand car dealers. It was one of these, Stanley Setty, whose dismembered body was dumped into the

marshes of the Thames estuary from an aeroplane in 1949.*
It is said that in this small quarter of London there is a known
criminal population of well over a thousand; but that may
well be too modest an estimate. The quarter has some of the
characteristics of a small town. Everyone knows everyone else.
Strangers are instantly recognised as such. News travels fast.
The police, however, unlike those of most small towns, go
about in pairs. Crime here is not a petty affair of pilfering from
parked cars or slot machines, but of safe-blowing and armed
bank hold-ups, of smash-and-grab raids and big jewel robber-
ies. It is a place where a girl can easily get to know too much,
and end up needing plastic surgery; or even on a police mor-
tuary table.

It is understandable that she should want to move to Mayfair where the money is better anyway and life is more
light-hearted. Besides, the humourless attentions of the 'push-
up mob' are not the only occasional occupational hazard she
has to face, especially if she works in the older Franco-Italian
section. Many of the stocking murders are committed there.
Old Compton Street, just behind Shaftesbury Avenue, has a
quite remarkable record in this respect. Perhaps it has something to do with the proximity of the theatres; the psychotic
comes to town, has dinner, sees a good show (or perhaps a bad
one) and then, feeling like strangling someone with a silk
stocking, moves off into near-by Soho to find a suitable subject.

* By Brian Donald Hume, tried at the Old Bailey for Setty's murder. He
succeeding in convincing the jury that he had disposed of the body in this way
under the impression that he was getting rid of some printing equipment for
three forged coupon operators named Max, The Boy, and Greenie. He was sentenced to twelve years' imprisonment as an accessory. When he came out, he took
the novel step of selling a full confession to the murder to a newspaper. He could
not be tried again, of course. He went to Switzerland and soon committed
another murder. He was convicted there and is now serving a life sentence.

There are signs, though, of a change. The Notting Hill Gate district, well west of Mayfair, is getting some of this trade nowadays. On the whole, murderers are a conservative lot; but, where sex-crimes are concerned, there has always been a westward trend. Seventy years ago practically all murders of this kind took place in the East End; more specifically in the boroughs of Stepney and Poplar and adjacent to their main traffic arteries, the Whitechapel and Commercial Roads.

If, for the suburban Londoner, the words 'West End' create a vision of wealth, gaiety, luxury and grace, the words 'East End' conjure up the very opposite—poverty, misery, squalor and violence. Nowadays, neither vision is very close to reality, for the West End is meretricious, and the East End has vitality and pride. But seventy years ago things were different. Then, the slums of Whitechapel and Spitalfields were horrible, and most of those who lived in them could make existence tolerable only by getting drunk.

This was the hunting ground that Jack the Ripper chose.

There have been many mass-murderers with bigger scores. Peter Kürten, the Düsseldorf sadist, killed ten and seriously injured over thirty-four; Doctor Palmer of Rugeley poisoned fourteen; William Burke, the Edinburgh Irishman, sold the bodies of sixteen victims; Fritz Haarman, the 'Ogre of Hanover,' was convicted of twenty-seven murders; Petiot, as we have seen, claimed sixty-three. Yet, Jack the Ripper, whose known killings total a modest six, is probably the most famous of them all.

Possibly, because he was never caught, nor even positively identified.

It all began in the early hours of the morning of August 7, 1888, on the stairway of a tenement house called George Yard Buildings in the parish of Spitalfields.

At 2 a.m. a couple named Mahoney returned to their room in the Buildings. Mrs Mahoney then went out to buy some fish and chips for supper. Both were comparatively sober. Neither of them saw anyone on the stairway.

An hour and a half later, another occupant of the Buildings, a cab-driver named Albert Crow, returned home from work. On his way up the dark stairs he noticed a figure lying on the first landing. He found nothing unusual in this. There *was* nothing unusual about it. He went up to bed.

At 5 a.m. another man, John Reeves, left the Buildings to look for work. There was some dawn light on the stairway now. He could see that the figure was lying in a pool of blood. He was a respectable man, so he decided to tell the police about it.

The body (for she was already dead) was that of Martha Turner (35) a married woman living, as a common prostitute, apart from her husband. She had lodged in Star Place, off the Commercial Road. The police doctor found thirty-nine deep stab wounds in the body, nine in the throat, the rest in the breasts and abdomen. At least two different knives had been used.

The discovery of this, the first of the Ripper murders, is described in some detail, not because it was specially interesting in itself, but because it is necessary for an understanding of the case of Jack the Ripper to appreciate the circumstances in which the crimes were committed. There were no street lights in the neighbourhood, no stairway lights. The sight of someone lying motionless on a public stairway (or indeed anywhere else) would excite no concern. It would be assumed that the person was drunk or asleep, or both. Not even the fact of the murder aroused much interest. There had been a lot of murderous assaults that summer in Spitalfields; there always were in the warm weather. In April, another prostitute, Emma

Smith, had died from one of them. The only novelty about the murder of Martha Turner was the extent of the mutilations, and even that was attributed to an attack by several men. That had been how Emma Smith had died.

It was the second Ripper murder that sounded the alarm.

At 3.45 a.m. in the morning of August 31, a man walking down Bucks Row,* Whitechapel, saw what he thought was a tarpaulin lying in the gutter. He was a cart driver, and the idea of acquiring a spare tarpaulin interested him. He crossed the road and took a closer look. He then saw that this was no tarpaulin, but a woman, dead drunk or just dead. At that moment another man came along and the two examined her. They found that her throat was cut and called the police.

The body was soon identified as that of Mary Nicholls (42) a prostitute who slept in common lodging houses. She had last been seen alive, and very drunk, at 2.30 a.m. It was the police surgeon who found that, in addition to the throat wounds which had caused death, the body had been almost completely disembowelled. At the inquest, he stated that, in his opinion, the crime had been committed by someone with a knowledge of surgery; and, moreover, by the same person who had killed Martha Turner. He could speak with some certainty, for by the time the inquest on Nicholls was held, the third murder had already been committed.

The victim this time was Annie Chapman (47), a widow. She, too, was a prostitute and she, too, lived in doss houses. At 2 a.m. in the morning of September 8 she arrived half drunk at a sixty-bed house in Thrawl Street, Spitalfields. The keeper of it refused to let her in as she did not have fourpence to pay for a bed. After arguing for a bit, she went away to earn the fourpence.

* After the Jack the Ripper murders, the name of Bucks Row was changed to Durward Street.

'Don't let my doss,' she called to the keeper as she went. 'I'll soon be back with the money. See what a fine bonnet I've got. I shan't be long.'

Her dead body was found four hours later in a yard behind 29 Hanbury Street, near Spitalfields Market. Her throat was cut and she had been disembowelled. It was not until a full post-mortem examination had been made, however, that it was discovered that the murderer had, with some skill, removed one of the internal reproductive organs.

The news, published with a wealth of medical detail that no paper would dare to print nowadays, shook Victorian England to the core. The whole thing was inexpressibly shocking. The very fact that the victims were all of the 'unfortunate' class touched the guilt-laden Victorian mind in a most sensitive area. The notion that the man responsible for these atrocities might be a surgeon; an educated, professional, respectable person, instead of a boozy brute of a labourer, was just as disturbing.

The East End was in a turmoil. This may seem surprising. After all, they were used to violence. Why should they get so excited about the deaths of these three wretched drabs?

Part of the trouble was that they could not yet realise that the murderer was confining his attentions to women of one particular kind. Everyone felt threatened. But even when the pattern of the murders became clear, a deeper horror still remained. The violence to which they were accustomed was that of relatively simple people. The fit of anger, the involuntary clenching of a fist or the seizing of a throat, the bash over the head, the clawing, snatching, kicking kind of violence— that they understood. Their forefathers had yelled and capered with the mobs at Tyburn while the executioner disembowelled the King's enemies. In their youth, the middle-aged among them had flocked to Newgate for a hanging. They understood the lust for cruelty and they understood the rage to kill. What they did not understand was madness—madness with intelligence. In fear already bordering on panic, they looked about for someone to accuse.

Their first choice fell upon a Polish Jew called John Pizer. He was known locally as 'Leather Apron,' a name to which the newspapers had no difficulty in imparting a sinister ring. It was said that he had been going about with blood on his hands brandishing long knives and threatening people, and that everyone went in terror of him. In fact, he was a harmless shoe-maker (and, not unnaturally, wore a shoe-maker's leather apron) with the sort of wild appearance and eccentricity of manner which sometimes goes with feeble-mindedness. As much for his own protection and a desire to placate the public as from a serious suspicion of his guilt, the police arrested and investigated him. At the adjourned inquest on Annie Chapman he was formally cleared. Other suspects were speedily found—a slaughterman, an inoffensive half-wit, a German named Ludwig—and as speedily had their innocence established. Exhibitionists made the usual false confessions. Public indignation began to focus on the police. The Commissioner at the time was Sir Charles Warren, a singularly pig-headed martinet who had regimented Scotland Yard into a state of wooden inadequacy that was becoming a public scandal. Even Queen Victoria felt strongly about it. She described herself as 'much upset' by the murders and thought that the police should 'employ more detectives.'

It was at this tense moment that the murderer (the title 'Jack the Ripper' had not yet been coined) brought off his most sensational *coup*. On September 30, in the space of less than an hour, he murdered two women.

The first, Elizabeth Stride (45), was killed in a small yard at the back of a house in Berner Street, Whitechapel. Just before

1 a.m. the driver of a small cart who stabled his pony in the yard, drove in at the end of his day's work. Suddenly, the pony shied and the driver jumped down to control it. He soon found that what had startled the animal was the body of a woman with her throat cut. Blood was still pumping from the wound. There was no mutilation this time. The murderer had only just that very moment killed. Almost certainly he was still in the yard. When the driver ran for help the murderer walked away.

He did not walk far.

Mitre Square is about fifteen minutes from Berner Street. At 1.45 a.m. a policeman flashing his lantern into the dark corners of the Square saw the body of Catherine Eddowes (45). Earlier in the evening she had been picked up helplessly drunk by the police and left in a cell to sleep it off. By 1 a.m. the police cells had been getting crowded (it was Saturday night) and, as she was by then sober enough to walk, the police had told her to go. A few minutes later she met the Ripper. Evidently, the interruption of his work in Berner Street had irritated him, for her body was so badly mutilated that it was some time before she could be identified. And the Ripper had added a flourish or two to his work this time. He had nicked her lower eye-lids with his knife; he had also neatly removed her left kidney.

The following day the Central News Agency revealed that on September 27 they had received a letter signed 'Jack the Ripper' saying that 'in the next job I will clip the lady's ears off and send them to the police.' They also announced that they had that morning (a few hours after the double murder) received a bloodstained postcard with the following message written on it in red ink:

I was not codding, dear old Boss, when I gave you the tip. You'll hear about Saucy Jacky's work to-morrow. Double event this time. Number one squealed a bit; couldn't finish straight off. Had no time to get ears for police. Thanks for keeping last letter back till I got to work again.

Coming on top of the double murder, the effect of these communications on the public was shattering. The expert opinion now is that both letter and postcard were the work of a practical joker; but at the time they were taken very seriously indeed. For, not merely did they give the murderer a name; they also suggested that the police were helpless. In fact, Scotland Yard had by now taken extraordinary precautions to prevent further murders. Big reinforcements of uniformed and plain clothes men had been poured into the East End rabbit warren. Patrols of vigilantes had been organised. Hundreds of suspects had been investigated. On the night of the double murder there had been two special constables within three hundred yards of the crime in Berner Street; and the policeman who found the body of Catherine Eddowes at 1.45 a.m. had been inspecting the lonely Mitre Square at intervals of fifteen minutes all through the night. As late as 1.30 a.m. he had found the Square empty. But there were three entrances to it and a maze of unlighted alleys and passageways all round. In fact the area was almost impossible to patrol effectively. Anyone who experienced the war-time London black-out will be inclined to sympathise with the Commissioner.

At the time he had no sympathy at all. The public was alarmed and it wanted action. The only action that the Commissioner had taken so far had been to conduct a trial of police bloodhounds on Tooting Common. The results were unfortunate. All the bloodhounds lost themselves and had to be tracked down by policemen. Amid the storm of angry derision which greeted the news of this fiasco, there were loud demands for Sir Charles' resignation.

In the end he did resign. Jack the Ripper must be the only murderer who ever succeeded in driving a chief of police out of office.

He waited five weeks before striking again.

The sixth victim was Marie Jeannette Kelly and she differed from her predecessors in three significant respects. She was young (24) and she was, despite her heavy drinking, still attractive. Unlike the other women, too, she had a room of her own on the ground floor of a place called Miller's Court, off Dorset Street* by Spitalfields Market. It was in this room that the murder was done, and for once Jack the Ripper had no fear of interruption. At 10.45 a.m. on November 9 someone happened to look through the window of the room and raised the alarm. By midday the London evening newspapers were bringing out special editions. By the afternoon all London had the details of the crime. Marie Kelly had died, as had the others, with her throat cut; but with time and privacy at his disposal, Jack the Ripper had acted out a terrible fantasy. The body of Marie Kelly had been almost completely dissected and the parts arranged methodically, with a kind of ritual precision about the torso.

That was Jack the Ripper's last murder.

There have been many theories put forward as to his identity and fate. Here are three of the commonest:

1. *The 'mad doctor' theory.* He worked in a London hospital, became a religious maniac and set out to destroy the wicked. He ended by committing suicide.

2. *The 'madness in high places' theory.* He was a member of a well-known and powerful family, and managed to conceal his ghastly propensities until, completely unhinged by the final murder, he gave himself away and was hurried off discreetly to a private hospital. There, he later died, a raving lunatic.

* Re-named Duval Street after the murder.

3. *The avenger theory*. He was a famous surgeon who set out to find and destroy Marie Kelly, the prostitute who had given his beloved only son syphilis. The other five murders were committed in the process of tracking her down (there could be no witnesses to the fact that he had made inquiries about Kelly) and the mutilations were to make the murders appear to be the work of a madman. He removed the internal organs for his private collection of pathological specimens. This quaint theory has been supported by a 'confession' alleged to have been made by the surgeon on his death-bed in South America.

Most of the other theories are on a similar level. It was the sudden cessation of the murders that presented the theorists with their knottiest problem. Modern psychological medicine would probably find that the least perplexing aspect of the case. During the last fifty years a great deal had been discovered about schizophrenia, and the Ripper murders would probably be diagnosed now as a case of 'fugue.' It is even possible that after the murder of Marie Kelly, Jack the Ripper never again knew of that passage in his life. There was something climactic and final about those incredible elaborations. Perhaps, having achieved an apotheosis of horror, he had at last exorcised the evil that had haunted him.

But what did he look like?

We can be quite certain of two things; he looked ordinary, and he looked harmless. Admittedly most of his victims were more or less drunk, but there was a panic in the streets then, and poor Annie Chapman in her new bonnet would have to feel very safe before, doss or no doss, she went with a dubious stranger into the blackness of the yard behind 29 Hanbury Street. And when Catherine Eddowes met him, he had come straight from killing Elizabeth Stride by cutting her throat. There would, inevitably, be blood on his clothes. Moreover, he had very nearly been caught by the sudden arrival of the man with the pony cart. Yet, to Catherine Eddowes, whom the police had thought sober enough to look after herself, he must have appeared normal and inoffensive. Probably, he was a local man, long known to all of these women and considered safe. One thing that seems unlikely is that the Ripper had the voice or manner of an educated Englishman, a 'toff.' Such a man would have been immediately suspect. Besides, surgeons are not the only ones who can dissect a body. Some butchers, too, have very skilful hands; and their eyes as they bend to their work are no less compassionate.

The face of murder, indeed, is more often bland than brutal, and a smile comes more readily to its lips than a snarl. Anyone who needs to be reminded just how unlike murderers real murderers look, should go to Madame Tussaud's exhibition of waxworks just off Baker Street. There, down below in the Chamber of Horrors, are London murderers by the dozen—Heath, Christie, Haigh,* Brides-in-the-Bath Smith, Chapman, who poisoned barmaids, Mrs Pearcey, who wheeled her victims' bodies through the streets of London in a pram, Crippen, Sheppard, who hanged at Tyburn, Dougal of the Moat Farm House—as infamous an assembly as you could wish for, and one of which Londoners are naturally, if furtively, proud.

The price of admission is only four shillings. For the timid it is quite the safest way of seeing criminal London; but only the *safest* way. It is not the most reassuring. There is something very familiar about some of the faces. Can it be something in the faces of the other Londoners standing beside you? I shall be glad of your opinions.

* In one of his own suits, jauntily bequeathed by him to Madame Tussaud's before his execution.

Other Pieces

1

Spy-Haunts of the World

A Realistic Guide for the Romantic Traveller

'Where can I see some real international spies?'

How often does one hear that simple question asked; and yet how rarely nowadays does one hear a well-informed reply. In a society devoted almost as enthusiastically to the diffusion of information about itself as it is to devising the means of its own destruction, this may seem incredible. But it is so. Useless to ask your travel agent. He just does not know; and if his nervous smile does not admit the fact at once, his mumbled references to Berlin and Vienna will very soon do so. The guide books, so helpful where food and architecture are concerned, do not even acknowledge the existence of spies.* Even the great public libraries have no up-to-date intelligence on the subject.

Why?

It is tempting, of course, to attribute this state of affairs to the inhibiting influence of some Higher Authority; and I know several experienced spy-spotters who are convinced that they are up against a world-wide conspiracy of silence organised by the spies themselves. Personally, I doubt this. True, international

---

* For example: in the current Michelin Guide, the town of Vincennes is briefly described with references to restaurants, a castle (with dungeon), a zoo and numerous garages. No reference whatsoever is made to the numerous spies, including Mata Hari, who have been executed there before firing squads.

spies do not like being spotted; if they did there would be neither point nor pleasure in spotting them; but the theory of conspiracy implies a spirit of co-operation, a readiness to join loyally with one's fellow men for a common good that is entirely foreign to all that is soundest in the international tradition.

No. The lamentable fact is, I think, that during the past decade the good, old-fashioned international spy, the vintage professional secret agent, has become so rare in the Anglo-Saxon countries that there has been a tendency to assume that the species is virtually extinct everywhere.

The assumption, mistaken though it is, is understandable. Try to think of one Anglo-Saxon spy trial during the last few years in which a real international pro. has been involved. You will find it difficult. Dissident scientists and technicians have no place in the spy-spotter's notebook; and mere venality does not make a traitor into a professional spy as we like to understand the term.* In the English-speaking areas this is the day of the amateur.

His unfortunate triumph has undoubtedly been due in the main to the need, where information about nuclear warfare is concerned, for special academic qualifications. If you want the secret of the new atomic warhead detonator, it is no use employing a man who may steal the plans of the kitchen equipment for the new canteen by mistake. There are, of course, a few professional spies with university educations, but not many of them have Ph.D.'s in physics, and it must be admitted frankly that a pass degree in the humanities or the ability to state Boyle's Law is just not good enough, even for

---

* The accepted definition of a professional spy is this: one who, having been born a citizen of country A, is employed by country B to spy on country C, or vice versa, or both, is domiciled in D, and holds a passport from E. He, or she, pays income tax in none of them.

work in the radar field. Sooner or later, American and British spotters will have to face the bitter fact that, in future, if they want to see active professional spies operating in their natural surroundings, they will have to go abroad to do it.

And they will have to go soon. It is said, I know, that there are still plenty of good hunting-grounds to be explored; and, admittedly, in the Mediterranean basin, the Middle East and South-East Asia, the situation for spies is not wholly impossible. In most of these areas the inhabitants can as yet do nothing about technical weapon development anyway, so that spies may still deal happily in the traditional items of military intelligence—numbers and movements of troops, locations of secret airstrips and ammunition dumps, thicknesses of armour plating, fire power, mobilisation plans, counter-espionage arrangements, states of readiness, plans of attack, anti-submarine boom defences, minefields and so on. And there are still, thank goodness, a few places where a good cover story and a well-forged passport are of more use to a man than a familiarity with the quantum theory. But for how long can this state of affairs last?

The truth is that life is not easy anywhere for the professional spy these days. At one time all you had to do if you wanted to spot spies was to take the Simplon-Orient Express from Paris to Istanbul. The second-class restaurant car was full of them, and identification was easy. You just took note of the travellers who had no trouble at all with passports or customs, and those were the spies.

Now it is very different. Not long ago, the *Observer* quoted an Orient Express Pullman attendant on the subject of immigration and currency restrictions.

'Even during the war,' this authority stated ruefully, 'we had the usual number of spies going back and forth, but now even spies cannot get the necessary travel permits.'

Happily, some of the more stultifying restrictions have since been eased, but it is still difficult to move from country to country in Eastern Europe, while in some areas of Asia the difficulties of getting a visa are further complicated by a regulation that makes it necessary to get the visa itself visa'd. I shall return to this development when I discuss the special problems of spies in Indonesia. My point here is that freedom of movement is the life blood of espionage and that restrictions that are merely irksome for the spy-spotter, may be positively unhealthy for the spy himself. We should be grateful that, in the face of so much discouragement, so many spies are prepared to carry on.

One more thing before we set off for the hunting grounds. The honest spy-spotter merely looks. He does not touch. Photography is permissible if the spy is foolish or slow-footed enough to permit it. Challenging is not allowed; neither is shadowing. Both have been found dangerous.

The unforgivable sin is to become officious.

I heard of one case which makes the blood run cold. The man was in Cairo on government business. Finding himself with time on his hands he naturally began spotting, and, beginner though he was, he very soon 'found.' A few days later he was dining with an Egyptian government official and actually *told* him. As a result the find was arrested. He was certainly a spy, and also badly wanted by the police for gold smuggling. And the worst of this abominable little story is that, while one cannot but feel saddened and disgusted by the wanton destruction of a good spy, one cannot help envying the vandal who was able to check his score so very conclusively. Of course, positive identification of that order comes only once or twice in a lifetime. I have had only one so far and though it happened as long ago as 1937, I still think of it with gratitude

and affection; though not, as you will see, without some
bitterness, too.

I was convalescing after an illness and the doctor advised a
few weeks rest in the sun; so I decided to take a boat and go to
Tangier.

From a medical point of view, Tangier was an idiotic choice.
The Spanish Civil War was in progress at the time, and, of
course, the international zone of Tangier had a frontier with
Spanish Morocco. In 1937, all sorts of rearguard actions were
still being fought in the city; and not only in terms of undercover work, of kidnappings and discreet assassinations. The
peace of the warm, soft nights was constantly shattered by the
sounds of rival political bands fighting gun battles in the
streets. The walls and mirrors in those dingy little cafés down
the Petit Suk were pock-marked and starred with bullet holes,
while on the chairs outside, gloomy looking Arabs sipped
mint tea and fingered the revolvers beneath their djibbahs.
The week before I arrived, a party of armed sailors from a
foreign destroyer in the harbour had actually marched ashore
and attempted to seize the Spanish (Loyalist) post office. After
a three-hour siege, they had been driven off by machine-gun
fire from the post office and retired with their wounded to
the destroyer; but it was rumoured that a German pocket
battleship would arrive the following week to do the job
properly. The place was not restful.

I spent most of the days on a beach east of the harbour. The
sun glared brassily on the white sand and sometimes there was
a strong, hot breeze that shrivelled the skin and brought a
feeling of blisters to the lips. On those days the sea looked
inviting, but the doctor had told me not to swim, and usually
I sat in the shade of one of the ramshackle wooden cafés
dotted along the foreshore.

The most frequented of them was owned and operated by a woman whom I will call 'Annette.' The café itself, although it had a gayer name, I will call '*La Voile Blanche*.'

It was a square matchboard building containing a rickety bar counter, a kitchen, and, at the back, Annette's bedroom. The *terrasse* in front consisted of a wooden porch with a plaited bamboo roof. Beneath it, standing crookedly in the soft sand, were a few iron tables and some bentwood chairs. The staff consisted of a half-witted Arab girl named Fatima with purulent conjunctivitis in both eyes. There were several cleaner, more inviting-looking places along that stretch of beach. That it was *La Voile Blanche* that attracted most of the custom was due entirely to Annette herself.

She was a plump, moon-faced, motherly woman of about forty-five with dark, curranty eyes, a ready smile, and a lot of drab brown hair that shed hairpins like dandruff in the breeze. I never discovered her nationality. At various times I heard her use five different languages with apparent fluency, and I have no doubt that she could express herself adequately in many more. Probably, she had a bad accent in all of them.

She found out all that she wanted to know about me within a few minutes of my arrival. First, in her rather sibilant English, she offered to look after my money and papers while I went in to swim. I said that I was not swimming. She said that the swimming was perfect. I explained that I was convalescent. In deep concern, she sent Fatima for one of *La Voile*'s two decrepit deck chairs, found a place for me in the shade and gave me a brandy on the house. Then, standing beside me and murmuring sympathetically, she shaded her eyes with her hands and peered out anxiously across the Straits of Gibraltar.

I had not noticed her doing this earlier, and now I asked her what she was looking for.

'My boys,' she said vaguely; 'my boys.' She pronounced it 'boyce.'

It was not until the next day that I discovered who her boys were.

At that time, Spanish waters were heavily patrolled by several European navies and 'courtesy' visits to the international port of Tangier were part of the cold war routine. As I have already noted, the courtesies were not always strictly observed, but the traditional formalities were, and it was usual, at any rate during the daylight hours, for a warship in the port to send a few trusted liberty men ashore. British, French, Italians and Germans were, of course, the most frequent visitors. The interesting thing was that, irrespective of nationality, most of the favoured few patronised *La Voile Blanche*. These were Annette's boys; and quite a high proportion of them were petty officers.

Why did they choose *La Voile Blanche*?

A British Engine Room Artificer explained why he came. *La Voile*, he said, was the only place in Tangier where you could get eggs and chips and a decent cup of tea. When I learned that for the Italians it was the only place in Tangier where you could eat *pasta* like mother made, and for the French the only place that served really eatable *casse-croutes*, copious yet reasonable in price, I began to understand why Annette gazed so often and so anxiously out to sea. The nationality of the visiting warships would determine her shopping list for the day.

Moreover, home cooking was not the only service that Annette offered her boys. She minded their valuables while they went swimming. She lent them swimming shorts and towels. She changed money for them. She mended their socks. It was even said that, in the case of one or two of the older men, she was not averse to a romp on the vast double bed that filled the room at the back. All, it seemed, that she demanded in return (apart from her modest charges for food and drink) was friendship; but friendship expressed in a particular way. Annette was lonely. What you had to do was to write to her now and then, and tell her how you were. She had quite a big post every day.

I wish I could claim that I 'spotted' Annette immediately. Unfortunately, I did not. But, as most experienced spotters will appreciate, things were very different then. Modern recognition aids would have left me in no doubt. Annette had the highest *louche*-rating I have ever encountered.

For those who are unfamiliar with the newest thought on spy-spotting, I should explain that all recognition now is based on what is called the '*louche* assessment figure' or '*louche*-rating' which works roughly on the same principle as the Beaufort scale for rating wind velocities.

Louche, you will recall, means literally, 'ambiguous.' Applied to persons, however, it has a special meaning hard to define. 'Questionable,' 'bogus,' 'meretricious'—none of them is quite synonymous. Broadly speaking the word suggests that the person to whom it is applied is suspect in a moral and/or social context, that he (or she) may have a faintly disreputable aspect, or a vice of which one would like to be forewarned. A prosperous *maquereau* sipping Vichy water in a Paris night club presents an unmistakably *louche* appearance (about seven on the scale); so does that attractive young woman whom nobody can remember inviting to join the party, and who borrowed ten shillings for a taxi home (*louche*-rating, two). 'Beware,' said Somerset Maugham, 'of the Englishman who speaks perfect French. He is either a confidence trickster or an embassy attaché.' '*Louche*-rating, five' might be the spy-spotter's comment on that one.

Here is how the scale is divided. Note that the assessments are purely metaphorical, merely denoting the degree of suspicion aroused for a given *louche*-rating. Thus, a woman could have a rating of six or seven and yet be quite irresistible.*

1. I wonder who pays for his/her clothes.
2. But I thought that he/she came with you.
3. There is something about him/her that I don't quite like.
4. That mouth of his/hers is quite peculiar.
5. I wouldn't trust him/her farther than I could throw him/her.
6. This one's straight out of the woodwork.
7. Thank goodness he/she is three tables away.
8. Better feel to see if my passport's safe.
9. I feel I ought to warn some authority about him/her at once.
10. I must get to a telephone.

Annette's final *louche*-rating was nine.

She had a passion for telling the story of her life and explaining how it was that she had come to be a *patronne* of *La Voile Blanche*. The interesting thing was that she never told the same story twice and yet seemed totally unaware of the fact. Of course, her 'boys' came and went and, presumably they either failed to notice the contradictions or did not care; but for three weeks I was a steady and fascinated audience. I soon came to know when a fresh version was brewing. It was always when business was slack. For perhaps ten minutes she would stand gazing out to sea, gloomily, like a ship-wrecked sailor who has given up hope of rescue. Then, she would turn away,

---

* Experience has shown that spies are generally to be found in the upper half of the scale. So are drug pedlars, confidence men, smugglers and other assorted crooks. It is for the spotter to discriminate. He must cultivate a 'nose' for spies. The scale is only an aid.

sit down beside me and send Fatima for the brandy and two glasses.

'It is too much for one woman,' she would begin. 'I shall sell the place. I have received some serious offers. It is incredible that a person in my position should be obliged to do this kind of work. But when one is no longer young one becomes a victim. When I was an attractive girl, my friend. . . .' And she was away.

I have said that the story was never the same. That is not quite so. The *shape* of the one she told me was always the same. It began when she was a girl, the cherished daughter of titled parents with big estates and peasants who adored them. But in common with other landowners they had had troubles. She had been affianced to a millionaire foreigner who was socially beneath her. For a time she had lived happily with him. She had had carriages, great wealth. Then, the rich bourgeois had revealed his true nature—drink, other women, perversions of every kind. She had refused to live any longer under his roof. There were some things no woman of spirit and breeding could support. She had preferred to starve. Parents dead. Estates confiscated. Gallant struggles. *La Voile Blanche.*

That was the pattern. The details, however, varied fantastically. The family estate had sprawled over the plains of Hungary, clustered round a Polish castle, stretched as far as the eye could see towards the hills of Greece and burgeoned under the friendly Bohemian sun. Papa had been a count, a *Freiherr*, a *chevalier*, a *von und zu*, a *Graf*, a Knight of the Holy Fleece. Mama had been distantly related to practically every royal house in Europe. The low-born millionaire husband had been a Frenchman, a German, an Italian, a Swiss, a Swede. He had made his fortune in soap, oil, 'contracting,' steel, munitions, scent, brandy. He had been surprised in every

compromising situation from plain adultery with a *fille de joie*
to the most intricate sado-masochistic orgies in the company
of—'but a woman cannot speak of such bestialities, you understand.' And he had struck her. Heavens, how he had struck
her! With a sjambok, with his ivory riding crop, with a knout,
with the back of his hand, the flat of his hand, his knotted fist,
the leather belt of his hunting jacket, a rawhide whip. 'Do you
not see the scar? No? In some lights one can still see it.'

I was an attentive, credulous listener. In a sense, every
writer of fiction is a liar; and the fact that he writes his lies
down in the hope of selling them for profit, instead of deliver-
ing them by word of mouth free of charge, does not, I think,
entitle him to be censorious. She was enjoying herself. I was
being satisfactorily entertained. I thought that we both
understood each other very well.

I was mistaken.

I had been sleeping in my deck chair one afternoon and
awoke to the sound of Annette's voice. Her audience was a
moody young sailor off the *Deutschland* and she was, of course,
telling him the story of her life; but to my astonishment I
realised that she was telling him one of a different pattern.
There were no noble parents, no vast estates, no carriages, no
rich foreign husband. This one was about a Little Nell of the
Vienna slums, or someone out of a German edition of *Little
Women* edited for publication by the brothers Grimm. I
listened fascinated. 'Often,' she was saying, 'we had only a
crust to eat. What milk we were able to get was saved, naturally, for the younger children.'

At that moment, she looked up and caught my eye.

For not more than a second, she looked disconcerted. Then,
and, I suppose, because she had been disconcerted, she made
a mistake. With a quick glance to make sure that the young
German was not watching her, she grinned at me and winked.

Now, the only thing that makes a liar tolerable is innocence. No matter how outrageous the fairy tale, she (or he) must believe in it *at the time*. The game of make-believe is then possible. The rules are tacitly accepted by both parties. The element of calculation is almost non-existent. To find, suddenly, then, that not merely has all the make-believe been on your side, but that you have been listening like a fool to someone skilfully pretending to be a pathological liar, is a shattering experience. What sort of mind is it that can contrive such a disguise? And what is it that has to be hidden?

I now know, of course, that the whole thing was really very simple. The clumsy lying was just another brush stroke in the synthetic character of 'dear, old, harmless, motherly Annette, with all her cock-and-bull stories about her past which you pretend to believe so that she'll forget to put those brandies on your bill, just as the other boys told you she would.' The wink was a mistake, as I have said, but it was a mistake of arrogance, not fear. She could have bluffed me easily with a wide-eyed stare. But, caught off balance, she responded instinctively, and pride in her own cleverness got in ahead of her sense of self-preservation. As *louche* as a wagonload of monkeys.

A few days later I learned the truth about Annette from a French radio operator off the destroyer *Simoun*, who had been one of her regular boys. I came across him sitting in a café in the town, and asked him why he was not down at *La Voile Blanche*. He told me that all the liberty men on his ship had been warned before going ashore that day not to go to Annette's. I asked him why.

'You know, of course, that she's a spy.'

'No.'

'I thought everybody knew.'

Every spotter will sympathise with my dislike of this odious young man. I asked him what he meant.

'Well, you know all those letters she gets every morning.'

'What about them?'

'She passes them on to the Russian consulate.'

'What for?'

'Movements of foreign ships. Gossip about what they have been doing and where they are going next. State of morale. Information about officers. Little scandals. You'd be surprised what some imbeciles will put in a letter.'

'You knew this all the time?'

'Of course. Only now the intelligence people have found out, too. So we have been ordered not to go there any more, and not to write to her. Myself, I never wrote, but it is boring not to have the use of the café.'

I was leaving early the next morning and had already said good-bye to Annette; but I could not resist the temptation to walk past *La Voile Blanche* to have another look at her.

The café was quite empty. She was standing in front of it, her hands shading her eyes as she gazed out to sea. *Simoun* was anchored only a quarter of a mile away from her, but she did not look in that direction. She must have guessed that something had gone wrong there. For her, no doubt, *Simoun* had now ceased to exist.

There was a strong mistral blowing. Her skirt was flattened against her big thighs and her hair streamed wildly as the wind tore at the hairpins. For no sensible reason that I could think of, I felt sorry for her.

For myself, I felt only disgust. I had spotted her all right, but not, unfortunately, as a spy. My own lame suspicion had been that she was in a drug smuggling racket of some kind. A really painful error. I have never had the heart to return to Tangier, though I understand that it remains very much a spotters' paradise. Perhaps Annette is still there. If so, I would like to think that she is now working for NATO. But I shall not trouble to find out. Nowadays, I prefer the other end of the Mediterranean.

The best way for a spotter to go to Istanbul is by sea. Denizyollari, the Turkish state shipping line, runs a regular service from Barcelona and Marseille. Their crack ship, *Ankara*, is particularly clean and comfortable. It calls at Genoa, Naples, and the Piraeus on the way. There are few tourists. Most of the passengers are travelling for business reasons, and there is magnificent spotting to be had. The crew is Turkish and highly respectable, while the captain has an unromantic passion for efficiency and punctuality; but some of the passengers are sure to have really exciting *louche*-ratings.

However, I must warn you that Istanbul itself is a troubling experience for the visiting spy-spotter. The inhabitants are so spy-conscious that one is made to feel like a tyro. The reason is that *everyone* in Istanbul has been spy-spotting passionately from the cradle on. Spies and spying are the staple subjects of polite conversation. The terrace of the Park Oteli looking out over the Bosphorus has one of the most exquisite views in the world and in the evenings the tables there are crowded. But nobody ever looks at the view. Everybody is too busy spotting and being spotted, and gossiping about the latest finds. The atmosphere is positively feverish.

The local rules, too, are confusing. In Istanbul there is one which allows anyone to be deemed *louche* who appears not to be *louche*. The results can be quite remarkable. On one occasion I was solemnly assured by intelligent Turkish friends that Douglas Fairbanks, Jnr., who had recently spent a few days there discussing a projected film about the life of Kemal Attaurk, was really a British [*sic*] spy, and that the film project was his cover story. Istanbul is definitely no place for the beginner.

Beirut is only an hour or two by air from Istanbul, yet how

different it is in feeling. In Istanbul the stones of Byzantium lie beneath your feet. Beirut is on the coast of what was once the land of Canaan, home of the greatest sea power and trading nation of the ancient world, the worshippers of Moloch—the Phoenicians. In Beirut, after nearly four thousand years, trading is still the mainspring of existence, and the spotter is advised to be careful. The *boîtes de nuit* there can always be relied upon to yield fascinating Levantine material; but to spot is to look and, in Beirut, to look generally means that you wish to possess. Unwary spotting can lead to both embarrassment and expense. It can also lead, I must admit, in pleasanter directions. If it does, you will not care whether you see any spies or not. Beirut is for the dilettante.

My own view is that for serious spy-spotting you have to go still farther east.

On no account should you miss Bangkok. For one thing it is the only capital city that I know of which is entitled to a *louche-* rating of its own. It is quite a satisfactory shock to discover that nearly all those glittering pagodas which give the place such a fine flavour of the mysterious East were built in the nineteenth century by Italian architects. Another distinct advantage is that, as Thailand is in the forward area of the Asian cold war, there are quite a lot of real spies and undercover agents operating there; a great help to the spotter, this. The Bamboo Bar of the Oriental Hotel and the foyer of the Trocadero Hotel are splendid hunting grounds. Late at night there is a place called 'Eve' which has much to recommend it.

The people of Bangkok are small, gay and sophisticated. However, they have a somewhat scatological sense of humour which the occidental may find disconcerting. Avoid people who know the language. Your personal dignity will be safer if you do not understand what the Thais are saying. Remember, too, that Bangkok is generally acknowledged to be the headquarters of the Asiatic 'blue' film producing industry, and high *louche*-ratings may be registered on all sides. There are, in addition, numbers of sinister looking Europeans. Do not be deceived by appearances. Many of them really *are* sinister.

It is unwise to stay too long in Bangkok. For one thing, so much good spotting will spoil you for other places. More serious, you may contract the Bangkok neurosis. The symptoms are unmistakable. A slight fever is followed by mild dysentery. Then, after a few days, you find yourself adopting a sort of Dali-esque attitude to life that is not far removed from whimsicality. This is the tertiary stage. Not only occidentals become infected.

In the Garden of the British Embassy in Bangkok there is a life-sized statue of Queen Victoria. When the Japanese army entered the city in 1942, they took over the Embassy as a military headquarters, and the local Japanese Commander gave orders for the statue to be boarded up. But after a few days in Bangkok, he found that something was troubling him. It was the statue. Queen Victoria it had been who, at the turn of the century, had recognised Japan as a great power. Japanese history books approved of her. No disrespect ought to be shown to her effigy. And yet, the political situation made it difficult. In the end he compromised. The boarding would remain, but in order to cause Her late Majesty the minimum of inconvenience, he gave orders for two small eye-holes to be cut in the boarding so that she could look out.

After Bangkok you had better go to Penang or Singapore for a day or two to recover your sense of proportion. And while you are doing that it may be as well if we have a spotter-to-spotter talk about Indonesia.

Theoretically, Djakarta, the capital, should have four stars in any spotters' handbook. It is in the right part of the world, the political situation is pure 'powder barrel,' while the number and diversity of the armed revolutionary groups operating there makes Central America seem like Sussex.

In practice, things are different. For a professional spy, Djakarta must be just about the most discouraging place in the world today. To begin with the business of getting in and out of the island of Java is made really difficult. I have already mentioned the visa problem. You get a visa for Djakarta in, say, London, and think you are cleared to enter. You are not. In Singapore, you have to get the visa visa'd at the Indonesian consulate. Then, when you get to Djakarta, the visa'd visa has to be visa'd again by three different immigration authorities before you are permitted to land. On the way out it is very much the same. For a stay of one week, my own passport collected two and half pages of visas involving the use of ten separate rubber stamps. How can a working spy be expected to find the time to forge all that stuff?

And that is not the worst he has to face. In the thirties, when Djakarta was Batavia and Dutch, the population was less than half a million. It has grown to approximately three million. Unfortunately, the housing and hotel situation has not grown with it. 'You can't sleep alone in Djakarta,' is the joke that greets you. And it is perfectly true. You can't. If you have plenty of pull with a member of the government you may get a bed in a hotel room, but it will have up to five other beds alongside it. All very well for a spotter perhaps, but one cannot seriously expect a professional spy to make his headquarters in a dormitory. Let him take a house or apartment, you say? But where? Even the Soviet Embassy has had to settle for a few rooms in the Hotel des Indes compound, and the first Ambassador to arrive from Ceylon had to go back to Colombo again until the Indonesian Government found him somewhere to live. Of course, one expects a good spy to be more resourceful than an ambassador, but when he has to apply his fine skills to the mundane business of flat hunting before he can even think of stealing a plan, who can blame him for becoming demoralised?

Bandung in West Java is only a little better. There, you can, if you work hard, get a hotel room to yourself for a couple of nights, but I cannot pretend that the spotting is worth it. While the Afro-Asian Conference was in session there, I have no doubt that the place was swarming with spies. When I was there, the only thoroughly *louche* characters were the *betchak* boys, who looked like government freedom-propaganda posters and muttered lewd advertisements for the local brothel in your ear as they pedalled you along the muddy streets. Even for a dedicated spotter, Indonesia is unrewarding.

South Vietnam has much to recommend it, and should have more. Unfortunately, Saigon seems to have contracted a mutation of the Bangkok neurosis.

It began with Graham Greene's novel *The Quiet American*, which was set in and near Saigon. Some of the action of the novel centres around a bomb explosion in a crowded café. It seems that there was just such an incident in Saigon during the troubles which Mr Greene used as the background of his story. Many were killed. The terrorists who caused the real explosion are unknown; but in the novel, an American undercover agent is responsible.

Now it is understandable that the Vietnamese should have liked this explanation of the incident; and they might reasonably have wondered if Mr Greene, who had been in their country, knew something that they did not; but their firm, happy insistence that the book is not fiction at all, but fact, is quite bewildering.

You cannot go anywhere in Saigon without the driver pointing out some landmark of *The Quiet American*. There is the café where the bomb explosion was made, this is the bridge by which the agent Pyle was found dead, that is where stood the restaurant at which Fowler and Granger talked (now it is destroyed), that is where the plastic bomb was prepared. In the torrid interior of a baby Renault taxi, the fantasy becomes infectious. Serious spotting is impossible.

Hong Kong is overrated in my opinion, and Macao only a little better. Smuggling, unless arms and ammunition are involved, rarely attracts the true professional.

Indeed, we have to face the facts that good spotting is getting harder to find every day, and that the situation is going to deteriorate still further unless something is done about it. Admittedly some professional spies still seem able to carry on, but I do not think it is generally realised that many of these are by now professionals in name only, mere part-time workers. If that trend continues we shall soon have nothing but amateurs.

I have said: 'Unless something is done about it.' What *can* be done?

My answer is simple. What was done about the American buffalo herds when they seemed to be approaching extinction? What was done about the elephants in Africa when the ivory hunters threatened to exterminate them? What was done about the golden plover when the English took to eating too many of its eggs?

Exactly! Men of goodwill got together, took the matter up at government level, had protective laws passed and established natural reserves in which the creatures could live and breed without further molestation.

The same can be done for spies.

What I propose is nothing less than the setting up of an International Spy Reserve, to be called 'The E. Phillips Oppenheim Memorial Park.'

Now it must be immediately apparent to everyone that

a project of this kind cannot be undertaken by a single government. Unilateral action in such a field would naturally give rise to all sorts of frustrating suspicions. The matter is obviously one for the United Nations. The appropriate agency would seem to be UNESCO, and, in fact, a small committee of spotters has been formed to draw up a preliminary plan for submission to that organisation.

A provisional site for the Park was the first item to be discussed and various suggestions were made. The final choice (which, however, had not yet received the approval of the French Government) was the Ile du Levant, off the coast of southern France near Marseille.

Splendidly situated in the Rade d'Hyeres, this charming Mediterranean island is about five miles long, its width varying between a half and three quarters of a mile. It has a small port, Grand Avis. The nearest mainland port is Le Lavandou, fifty minutes away by ferryboat. It is separated from the neighbouring island of Port Cros by a strait about half a mile wide. The climate is, on the whole, excellent; a little mistral, perhaps, but nothing serious. At the western end near the small village of Heliopolis, there is at present a large nudist colony. The important thing about the Ile du Levant, however, is that it is full of ruined buildings, old houses, chapels, an abbey, a missile testing ground, and, above all, a magnificent collection of *disused forts.*

Originally, the island was fortified, as part of an eighteenth-century coastal defence system, by Louis XIV's great engineer, Vauban. The forts were later modernised by Napoleon, and are still in reasonably good condition. Their appearance is superb. It would be a pleasure to spy on them.

It was these forts that decided the committee. With them, the Ile du Levant has everything spies need. Garrisons of disabled army veterans could easily be provided for the spies to outwit. Escapes by boat to the mainland could be made at dead of night without risk to neighbouring shipping (the main shipping lanes run outside the islands) and, more important, in absolute safety for the spies themselves. The French missile testing area seemed at first to present a security problem; but it was soon pointed out that, as the spies would not be rocket scientists, this could be disregarded. The only real drawback is the nudist colony. This would have to go. In the view of the committee it is absolutely essential that spies of impeccable quality are introduced for breeding purposes, and there must be no undesirable distractions. Besides, spies thrive on secrecy and the need for covering-up. The island is warm in summer, and the risk of the females being tempted out of their traditional black satin into bikinis, or worse, could not be accepted.

Among other proposals before the committee at the moment is one for classifying the spy population by vintages, and another for improving the breed by means of education. Under this latter scheme it might be possible at a later date to provide a small atomic pile for the advanced student groups to spy on.

But it is useless to go into too much detail at this stage. The main thing is to get the principle accepted, so that the work of collecting can begin. Some qualified spotters are convinced that if the present trend is allowed to continue, another ten years will see professional espionage practically extinct; that even now it might be difficult to assemble more than fifty really first-rate pairs.

If this is true, then we are facing a cultural disaster for which our children will not readily forgive us. The responsibility is ours, now.

There is not a moment to lose.

2

Monsieur Gaumont

He was on a Messageries Maritimes boat going from Marseille to the Far East.

It was winter and the Mediterranean was rough. For the first two days Monsieur Gaumont and his wife stayed in their cabin. On the third day I saw them on deck. She was in a long chair and he was tucking a rug round her.

She was young, dark, pretty, and very shy. He was in his late thirties, tall, thick-set and fair-haired with a small moustache. He exuded well-being; she looked a little wan and frail. He fussed over her, rearranging cushions, and she looked up at him with an adoring smile.

The purser told us that they were on their honeymoon. The jokes began. Then it had *not* been Madame's sea sickness which had kept the Gaumonts in their cabin. With that great ox of a husband to appease, no wonder the poor child looked frail.

As the days went by, other facts about the Gaumonts emerged. Although he was down on the passenger list as a Frenchman, they spoke together in German; she could speak no French. He was some sort of engineer. They were going to Saigon to live. He had been in Indo-China before; until now, she had never been out of Germany.

Soon, she began to learn a few words of French and her shyness abated a little. He was an enthusiastic deck-tennis player, and although his big body moved clumsily, it also moved swiftly. He was never without a partner or an opponent. His good humour was inexhaustible and his solicitude for her charming. They were a popular couple.

The second night out of Bombay the commandant's gala was announced. A special dinner was to be served. There would be gifts for the ladies, paper hats, competitions, prizes, dancing. Gentlemen were requested to wear evening dress.

In the tropics, this meant, for the ship's officers, white drill, for the French army officers among the passengers, khaki drill, for the civilians, a white dinner jacket with black tie.

It was a hot night and I postponed changing as long as I could. When at last I went up, most of the other passengers were already there. However, they were not, as I had expected, preparing for the festivities in the bar. The majority, all of them French, were out on deck, clustered in groups and staring at the commandant of the ship. He was a tight-lipped man and a fervent Gaullist. Now, white with anger, he appeared to be denouncing his first officer and the purser. 'It is an enormity, an affront,' he was saying.

I asked a French army captain what the trouble was. 'Gaumont,' he answered. 'In the bar. See for yourself.'

I went into the bar and ordered a drink.

Gaumont was sitting with his wife at the bar, chatting, in his usual good-humoured way, to an elderly Tonkinese couple. Some of the non-French passengers were there, too. I was puzzled for a moment. The only thing I could see wrong with Gaumont was that he seemed to have taken the request for formal dress too literally.

He was wearing a short white jacket of the kind worn by officers in some service messes, and he was wearing medals. I recognised a Croix de Guerre with palms, among others that I did not know. The decorations were suspended along one of those loops of thin gold chain which Frenchmen commonly use for dress miniatures, and fastened across his jacket lapel. None of the other men was wearing medals, and obviously Gaumont was being rather silly, but I could not see why the French should be so incensed about it.

Then, he moved slightly and I did see. On his breast, immediately below the row of miniature French decorations, was a full size German Iron Cross.

The gala was not an unqualified success, although the Gaumonts appeared to enjoy themselves immensely. He seemed to be quite unaware of the hostility he had aroused. That he had not been unaware, I learned a day or two later. On the commandant's orders the purser had requested him to remove the Iron Cross. Gaumont had refused on the grounds that, as he had earned it, he was entitled to wear it. He had earned the Croix de Guerre and was entitled to wear that, too. He told the purser why.

He had been a submarine officer in the German Navy at the beginning of World War II and had earned his Iron Cross sinking Allied shipping. Early in 1940, however, his submarine had been depth-charged by a French destroyer and blown, disabled, to the surface. He had been picked up and put in a prisoner-of-war camp at Lorient in Brittany. He had escaped once and been recaptured. When French resistance to the German Army's advance had begun to collapse, he had escaped again, this time successfully, and made his way to Spain.

There, presumably, he had been interned. I say 'presumably' because there was a gap of five years in the story here. I wondered if he had been offered a chance of repatriation by the Spanish authorities, and had, for some reason connected with his old life in Germany, rejected it. But he was not disposed to discuss that period of his life. In 1945, he joined the French Foreign Legion in North Africa and was posted, after training, to Indo-China. He remained there throughout his two periods of service in the Legion, and rose to the highest rank attainable by a legionnaire who is not a Frenchman, that of warrant officer.

A foreigner, whatever his nationality, who has done long-term service in the Legion, and has a record with it of good behaviour, may, if he wishes, take French citizenship upon his discharge. The German had elected to do so. He had also changed his name to Gaumont at that time. He had then gone back to Europe.

He had not stayed there long, however. By-passing France, he had made for West Germany. In two months he had not only found the job he wanted to do, but also met, wooed and won his German wife. Now, he was on his way back to Indo-China. His job was a good one. He was to be sole agent there for a German arms manufacturer.

The boat stayed three days in Saigon, and the Gaumonts lived on board while he made arrangements ashore to lease an apartment and an office. They were obviously looking forward keenly to their new life. Only one thing seemed to trouble him; the problem of buying a car. It was difficult, he told me. I could not see why. There were brand-new Peugeots, Renaults and Citroens by the dozen on the dock, and one had heard that they were being shipped elsewhere for lack of buyers. He shook his head doubtfully. I concluded that his other expenses ashore had left him short of money.

The day before the boat sailed I was going to lunch with some friends who lived on the other side of the city. I was taking the only taxi on the rank at the dock gate when he came out of the Port Commandant's office and hurried over. He was breathless and obviously flustered about something. He asked if I would mind sharing the taxi with him. He had to get to the Cathedral at once.

As we started off, I tried to think of some way of satisfying my curiosity. Was he going to Mass? Not at that time of day, surely. Confession, then? I could not really believe it. To pick up his wife? But I had seen her on board as I had left. And why the urgency? In the end, I decided to ask him.

'I've only seen the Cathedral from the outside,' I said. 'What's it like?'

He shrugged. 'I don't know. Like most cathedrals, I suppose.' He leaned forward impatiently as the driver braked to avoid a cyclist, and told him to go faster. Then, he gave me a harassed glance. 'There's a garage along the street beside the Cathedral,' he explained. 'The Port Commandant says they had a Mercedes Two-Twenty for sale yesterday. I wouldn't like to miss it. It's just what I need.'

I still wish I knew why he became a Frenchman.

3

The Legend of the rue Royale

I go off to Maxim's
Where fun and frolic beams,
With all the girls I chatter,
I laugh and kiss and flatter
Lolo, Dodo, Joujou,
Cloclo, Margot, Froufrou!
For surnames do not matter,
I take the first to hand.

The Merry Widow
FRANZ LEHAR

There are probably as many cafés, restaurants and night clubs in the world called Maxim's as there are hotels with the borrowed word 'Ritz' in their names. Certainly, there has never been another restaurant about which so many stories have been told.

Here is a recent example:

A young Frenchman, newly returned to Paris after his service in North Africa, is taken by a rich aunt to lunch at Maxim's. It is the first time he has ever been there and the aunt looks forward eagerly to sharing his pleasure in the experience. He remains silent, however, and in the end she is forced to ask what he thinks of it.

'The food is excellent,' he replies politely.

'Oh, the food.' She shrugs. 'Yes, it is good. However, one does not come to Maxim's merely for the food. It is the atmosphere. Do you not find it marvellously sympathetic?'

'Frankly, my dear aunt, I don't. The decorations are old-fashioned in an ugly way. As you would expect in so expensive a place, the women are well-dressed, but mostly—forgive me—they are not of my generation. The men are clearly rich, but what else have they to recommend them? The food is excellent, but you tell me that that is not the important thing at Maxim's. What is it then? To be seen here? I find such antique snobbery absurd and a little sad.'

The aunt bridles. 'North Africa has made you insensitive. You do not understand.'

'No, I don't. You will have to explain. Why do people still come to this place?'

'They come,' the aunt replies with triumphant simplicity, 'because it is a place where for sixty years people have been happy.'

Collapse of nephew, abashed.

Of course, he might have retorted that it is possible to hate as well as love in a restaurant, no matter how good the food; but stories about Maxim's never seem to end that way.

This is how the myth began.

In the early eighteen-nineties the ground floor of number three, rue Royale was occupied by an Italian ice cream merchant named Imoda, who specialised in something he called 'meat-juice ice cream.' He had, too, a defective sense of self-preservation. One fourteenth of July, he was tactless enough to decorate his shop with the German flag. The result was that a patriotic crowd stormed the place and wrecked it. Shortly after that he went out of business. No more was heard of him; nor, mercifully, of his meat-juice ice cream. In 1892, a waiter named Maxime Gaillard reopened the place as a café.

It was Maxime's first business venture and he had a partner named Georges. They had virtually no capital—a wine merchant, a brewer, and other suppliers had undertaken to give them credit—and things went badly from the start. The public did not want to sit in a café in the rue Royale, preferring the more convivial atmosphere of the Grands Boulevards. Within a year, the business had failed, Georges had gone, and Maxime had taken on two partners of a more formidable calibre, one a cook and the other a maître d'hotel. The cook was Chauveau. The maître d'hotel was Eugène Cornuché. In 1893, having redecorated the premises and purchased an assortment of chairs and tables at an auction, the new partners reopened the place as a restaurant. At the time it was fashionable to anglicise French names; so they called it, after the founder of the enterprise, 'Maxim's.' And there, for all practical purposes, Maxime Gaillard's connection with the establishment ended. He had contracted tuberculosis and two years later he was dead.

A number of explanations have been given for the rapid success of Maxim's. One story is that it was due to the intervention of a famous demi-mondaine, Mademoiselle Irma de Montigny. Weber's was then the accepted meeting place for what is now called (though not in France) 'café society.' It seems that one evening the maître d'hotel at Weber's neglected to keep a table for Irma. In a pet, she swept off down the street to Maxim's, and took all her friends with her. Another version has it that the popularity of Maxim's was due to the efforts of a sugar manufacturer, Max Lebaudy, who used to entertain wealthy men friends there. His own unerring taste in the selection of women companions for his guests was attributed to the management of Maxim's, who received in consequence a steady stream of valuable new customers.

That may be true. Certainly the Mademoiselle de Montignys and the Monsieur Lebaudys made their contribution to the character of Maxim's. But the real reasons for its eventual success were simpler. It was managed by two exceptionally shrewd and able men; and it was in the right place at the right time.

At the turn of the century, the Great Paris Exhibition ushered in that brief period of French social history which was to become known as *La Belle Epoque*. In many respects a legacy of the bounding, brassy, luxurious Second Empire, it yet had something peculiarly its own; at atmosphere of elegance, of lightness of heart and of serenity. It was the time of Paul Bourget and Pierre Loti, of Sarah Bernhardt and Edmond Rostand, of the young Proust and the young Colette, of Renoir, Matisse, Monet, Rodin, Vuillard and Toulouse-Lautrec. It was a time of gaiety. Above all it was a time of certainty, of confidence in a social order and of absolute belief that so splendid a state of affairs must be permanent. 'Frivolity,' a young man was told by the famous Hortense Schneider, 'is the secret of happiness. I have been a frivolous woman. I came from a frivolous period. Frivolous people are happy people. Take care, Monsieur, to remain frivolous all your life.'

In *La Belle Epoque*, if your name was in the Almanac de Gotha or you were very rich, or both, that was sound advice. It was also easy to take. A gentleman could begin by going to Maxim's.

Not, however, with his wife; nor with any other woman of his own social circle. 'When I passed Maxim's I shut my eyes as my mother had told me to do—it was no place for any self-respecting girl.' The writer of that sentence was no prim provincial demoiselle but the great Mistinguett of the fabulous legs and the Folies Bergères. However, her disapproval was not wholly righteous. 'That glittering assembly of demi-mondaines, with their money, their jewels and their royal lovers,' she went on resentfully, 'queened it over Paris society.'

And they did. People came from far and wide just to see the *grandes cocottes* of Maxim's in their plumes and jewels and voluminous silks, sipping champagne to the sounds of a string orchestra and the heady perfumes of syringa, patchouli and musk.

There was Carolina Otero, *La Belle* Otero, who used to appear so loaded down with the jewelled gifts of her admirers that it was said by the uncharitable that she had to be supported to her table.

There were Alice Gaillard and Manon Loty and Nine Desforets. There was Liane de Pougy, who sported two Arab servants and became the Rumanian Princess Ghika. There was Gaby Deslys, the lover of King Manuel of Portugal. There were Emilienne d'Alençon and Jeanne and Anne de Lancy and Cleo de Merode—they all had marvellous names. Sometimes it was even possible to catch a glimpse of the exquisite Lily Langtry as she hurried, veiled, from her closed carriage to a private room on the first floor, and a rendezvous with a future King of England.

Competition among the ladies was keen and feuds common. Emilienne d'Alençon became so irritated by *La Belle* Otero's massive displays of jewellery that she herself made a dramatic entrance one night wearing no jewellery at all, but followed by her maid carrying her jewel case on a velvet cushion. The joke was hilariously applauded. Otero seethed. But time brought her revenge. *La Belle* was able to retire luxuriously to her own villa in Nice. Emilienne d'Alençon married an impecunious jockey and sank into obscurity.

However, she must have been improvident. Most of the Maxim's ladies were able to feather their nests comfortably enough. With a male clientèle which included the Tsar Nicholas II, kings (Victor Emannuel II, Oscar of Sweden, Alfonso XIII, Leopold II), grand dukes (Vladimir, Boris, Michael, Dimitri), various princes, the wealthier nobility of Europe as well as a whole flock of ordinary millionaires, it was not too difficult. Maxim's was for the prodigal spender and, until the newcomer knew his own way about, the management was always there to help him.

For instance, Hugo, the head waiter, kept track of the ladies' various liaisons and entered the results of his observations in a little black book. Thus, the disposition and availability of any particular lady could be checked before overtures were made, so that mistakes embarrassing to both sides might be avoided. Some of the discreet notations employed by Hugo in his book became famous. 'RAF' meant 'nothing doing' (*rien à faire*). 'AF' (*à faire*) meant the opposite. 'PLM' (*pour le moment*) advised against any permanent arrangement, as did the disapproving 'FSB' (*femme seule au bar*), and the regretful 'E2A' (*entre deux âges*). 'YMCA' (*il y a moyen de coucher avec*) was a seal of approval, with reservations.

Eccentricity was tolerated unflinchingly. The Grand Dukes, fearsomely uninhibited men, could roister to their Russian hearts' content; and when an American, a Mr McFadden, ordered a nude girl covered with pink sauce to be served to his guests on a silver salver, not even an eyebrow was raised in protest. Unhappily, we have no record of the scene in the kitchen when the order was received, nor of the kind of pink sauce the chef decided to use; but the dish was duly served and Mr McFadden paid the bill.

The efficacy of Maxim's arrangements for its patrons' comfort sometimes had remarkable results. A provincial grocer who had made a fortune out of army contracts came to Paris for a week, without his wife, and went to Maxim's. The evening was a success and he kept on going to Maxim's. His wife did not see him again for three years. He only went home then because he was penniless.

In 1907 Eugène Cornuché and Chauveau sold out to a group of London business men who set up a British company, Maxim's Ltd, to take over. Gustave Cornuché, Eugène's brother, became manager. But nothing else changed. The gentlemen of Europe and America came and went; James Gordon Bennett, Louis Renault, Caruso, Chaliapin. The customers danced the *maxixe*, the tango and the one-step. True, there was some staff trouble; Rigo, the gypsy orchestra leader, eloped with the Princess de Caraman-Chimay (née Clara Ward, a beer heiress from Detroit); but it was easy enough to replace him. Maxim's became more and more glamorous. Franz Lehar wrote it into his operetta, *The Merry Widow*. Playwrights wrote plays about it—Feydeau with his *La Dame de Chez Maxim's*, Mirande with *Le Chasseur de Chez Maxim's*. Maxim's and *La Belle Epoque* flowered together.

The petals fell in 1914. During World War I, Maxim's, like an Edwardian matron, E2A, went into decline. As a meeting place for young Air Force officers on leave, it managed to preserve a certain gaiety, but nothing there was ever quite the same again. The names which decorate that period of its history are significantly drab: Mata Hari and Bolo Pasha, both executed at Vincennes on charges of espionage, Madame Humbert, the confidence trickster, and so on. Maxim's glamour had degenerated into notoriety.

The process continued after the war. The successors to Liane de Pougy and *La Belle* Otero were very much *femmes seules au bar*; the Grand Dukes had given place to paunchy business men from the Levant; and if the bar made money, the restaurant lost it. In 1932, a man named Octave Vaudable bought in a majority of the shares from the London company, and took over the management.

Like the original Cornuché, Vaudable was a man with imagination. A successful Paris restaurant proprietor of great experience, he had the wit to understand that the shares of Maxim's were worth more than the dismal statement of accounts appeared to indicate. What he perceived was the existence of a vast reserve of invisible assets: the twenty-year-old ghosts of *La Belle Epoque*. He set about making them work for him. After a period of trial and error he found the means.

Maxim's second period of prosperity began with the arrival there of Albert Blaser as maître d'hotel.

Albert came from Ciro's and was famous before he set foot in Maxim's. He had his own strict ideas of what the clientèle of a fashionable restaurant should be. He brought with him not only ideas but the clientèle, too. They fitted Maxim's perfectly, and the ghosts came out to welcome them. But ghosts on their best behaviour. No nude girls covered with pink sauce, no boisterous Grand Dukes smashing champagne glasses, no Hugo with his sinister black book, no *grandes cocottes* to trouble the respectable married woman dining sedately with her husband; just the cosy, pleasurable memories of those far-off things in their original setting. Maxim's had learned how to capitalise on nostalgia.

War came again, and Maxim's, still a British company, was placed by Hitler under the sympathetic supervision of Herr Horcher, a Berlin restaurant owner of appropriate distinction. Göring, Göbbels and other senior Nazis came to dine with the ghosts and be received by their representative, Monsieur Albert. Maxim's had acquired the status of an ancient monument.

It still retains it. For American tourists in the upper income brackets it is a 'must.' You are from Los Angeles? How nice! Let me be your guide.

The keepers of Maxim's today are Louis Vaudable (the son of Octave) and his wife Maggie, a law graduate of Lyons University. However, we shall not ask to see them. They are charming people, but very busy. In addition to owning sixty-five per cent of the shares of Maxim's Ltd, they also supply ready-cooked meals to Pan-American Airways and run a frozen sauce business in New Jersey. Perhaps we shall wave to them across the restaurant.

The big night at Maxim's is on Friday, when the women are in evening dress and the men must wear dinner jackets. It will be necessary, too, for you to reserve a table. I will meet you in the bar at nine-thirty.

The bar is upstairs above the restaurant, and is where the private rooms (no more of that) used to be. Beside it, there is a charmingly decorated dining-room called the Imperiale, much favoured by the younger set, and those who find the grandeur below a little stifling. I shall have a champagne cocktail. And, by the way, I want one thing clearly understood—the drinks in the bar (which are moderately priced) I shall pay for. You can pay the bill downstairs.

Well now, if you are ready, let us go down and face the music.

At the entrance we are met by the plump, pudgy Monsieur Albert.* His dewlaps quiver slightly as he greets us in fluent, faintly Cockney English, and makes up his mind which table he is going to give us.

The restaurant is divided into three parts; a small front room, a large back room and a broad connecting passage, with tables along both walls, called the 'Omnibus.' The back room

* Written four years ago.

is for celebrities, the nobility, the rich and the very fashionable; the Omnibus takes care of the less exalted; the front room is for the rest. At least, that is the theory. It is Albert who determines where you belong. It has been said, I know, that his decision has nothing whatever to do with your social standing or financial consequence, and that a five thousand franc note will get you a back room table right next to ex-King Peter of Yugoslavia, if that is where you want to be. This is a monstrous suggestion, and absolutely untrue. Only an envious cad in a badly cut suit, and without a five thousand franc note to his name, would make it.

However, we need not worry. Your wife is young and attractive and looking incredibly *chic* tonight in that little thousand dollar dress you bought her at Balenciaga's. Albert has an eye for glamour. She will be our passport.

We go in.

Eugène Cornuché decorated Maxim's in the style which we call *art nouveau*, but which the French perversely describe in English as 'modern style.' The walls are festooned wildly with loops and arabesques of some dark, bilious-looking wood, and writhing ornaments of lacquered brass. The lighting fixtures, too, are of lacquered brass, grimly fashioned into the shape of calla lilies. And there are the famous Cheret and Capiello murals. We pass one depicting a large, pale-pink lady about to dive into a river. We are now approaching the back room.

I said earlier that we were going to face the music. This was no idle figure of speech. The music—provided by a string orchestra which would be more at home playing selections from *The Tales of Hoffman* than the samba it is grappling with at present—*has* to be faced. It is deafening. For this discomfort, the acoustics of the back room are said to be responsible. It was the courtyard of the old house until Cornuché covered

it with a stained glass roof. The roof makes every sound rever-
berate. While the orchestra is playing, all conversation is
conducted by shouting or in sign language. As it is difficult to
talk for the moment, we may as well consider the gay cosmo-
politan crowd before us.

Over there between those two pillars is the famous table
number sixteen. Princess Margaret and the Duke and Duchess
of Windsor (Maxim's still has a weakness for royalty) get
number sixteen when they go to Maxim's. Tonight it is occupied by a party which includes Miss Marlene Dietrich. All,
except Miss Dietrich, are having a rough time, as there are no
less than four press photographers at work on her, and their
elbows are sharp. A middle-aged man at the next table is
getting furious because one of the photographers keeps butting
him.

Now who else is there of note? That decrepit-looking couple
over there are a French count and his countess. They are
regulars and fill up on champagne every night. That man with
hiccups in the corner is an obscure Irish peer. Mr Onassis, the
shipping magnate, you may not have met. As for the rest, I can
see that you have already noticed something familiar about
them. Exactly! They were all with you on the boat coming
over—the couple from Hagerstown, Maryland, that charming
pair from Muncie, Indiana, those two who are now bribing
one of the photographers to get them in a picture with Miss
Dietrich—you know them all. Of course, the women have
been to Dior and Balmain, and look different tonight, but the
men are just the same. That one on the dance floor who is
laughingly pointing an imaginary gun at his friend and making
clicking noises with his tongue; was it Texas he said he came
from?

Yes, except for the food, it is all very much like home.

When Metro-Goldwyn-Mayer made a film of *The Merry*

Widow, they asked Lorenz Hart to rewrite the lyrics. This is what he gave Jeanette MacDonald to sing:

> *Good-bye to you, Maxim's,*
> *I don't believe in dreams,*
> *The evening was splendid*
> *But now the play is ended.*
> *I give to you Joujou,*
> *Cloclo, Margot, Froufrou;*
> *The wine has lost its flavour*
> *I leave Maxim's to you.*

He must have dined there on a Friday.

4

The Magic Box of Willie Green

Brooke Street, in the City of London, lies off Holborn, amid the tangle of narrow lanes between the law offices of Gray's Inn and the diamond market of Hatton Garden. Nowadays, the greater part of one side of it is taken up by the pseudo-Gothic office building of an insurance company, but the other side is still very much as it was sixty-two years ago. There are small shops with offices above them and, at the far end, warehouses with loading platforms and wall derricks on the upper floors. It is a commercial street. At night it is silent and deserted.

The policeman who walked slowly along Brooke Street late one night in the February of 1889 must have been very bored. The fact that on the third floor of No. 24 there was a lighted window could not have interested him; he would have assumed automatically that it belonged to the office of some solicitor's clerk or bookkeeper catching up on arrears of work. It was not until well after midnight that the policeman entered history.

He was approaching the corner of Leather Lane, when he heard, coming from the darkness behind him, the sound of a door being flung open, a shout and then the quick scuffling of running feet.

He turned quickly. As he did so, he twisted the slide of his bull's-eye lantern and flashed the light in the direction of the sounds.

What he saw was a man running towards him; a short, fair, hatless man with a straggling moustache and a wild look. The man dashed up breathlessly.

'Come quickly, Constable!' he gasped. 'Come and see!'

The policeman was young, cautious and mindful of his training. 'Now just a moment, sir,' he began; but the short man had no time for explanations.

'No, no! Come and see! I've got to show you what I've done.'

The policeman tightened up inside. 'Something you've done?'

'Yes, that's it!'

The policeman began to walk back along the street. The short man capered ahead of him chattering excitedly.

'You see, I've only just this minute done it. And I don't mind telling you I was scared. But I managed it, and though I dare say it's very foolish of me, I feel I've just got to show someone.'

The policeman walked on grimly. He had never had a homicidal lunatic to deal with before, but this was how he had always imagined it would be.

'Of course,' the lunatic was saying, 'I'd like to show my wife, really, but she's not here now. And the joke is, Cousin Alfred didn't even know what I was doing.' He chuckled horribly. 'And now there he is, on the sheet, just as if he were alive. Here we are! It's upstairs!'

They had reached a dark doorway and the short man was standing aside for the policeman to enter. The policeman paused.

'Just a minute. Are you the owner of these premises?'

'Oh, no. I'm one of the tenants, the one who makes the smells. Friese-Greene's my name.'

'I see. All right. You lead the way, Mr Greene.'

'Yes, indeed. I'll go up and get everything ready for you.'

The man who called himself Friese-Greene clattered away up the dark stairs.

The policeman followed soberly. He was conquering his fears now. As long as he kept behind the man nothing much could happen. The phrases of the judge who would congratulate him on his courage and steadiness began to form in his mind. By the time he had reached the third floor, he had himself well in hand.

He crossed the landing to the doorway of the room with the light in it and looked in.

He had expected an office. What he saw was a cross between a workshop and a chemical laboratory. At a bench in the centre of the room, the madman was bending over a mechanism with a light in it which he was fitting into a box. There was a disagreeable smell in the room. The policeman looked round.

'Well,' he said, 'where is it?'

The man looked up. 'Where's what?'

'What you've done.'

'Sit down there a minute and I'll show you.'

The policeman looked round again, then sat down gingerly and watched his man.

He had finished with the mechanism now. He glanced at the policeman.

'Do you mind putting out your lantern, Constable?'

Reluctantly, the policeman twisted the slide of his lantern. The man reached up and extinguished the gas-light overhead. The only light in the room now came from the box.

'Now then, Constable! Look at that wall there.'

As he spoke a clicking noise came from the box and a rectangle of light appeared on a sheet stretched across the wall. Then, it darkened and in its place, grey and flickering, appeared the image of an avenue of trees and the figures of a man and a boy approaching. The man seemed to be only a foot or two away when he stopped, smiled in a puzzled way and pointed. Suddenly, he disappeared and in his place there was a picture of horse-drawn carriages going by against a background of trees. Then, that, too, disappeared and the sheet was blank again. The whole thing had lasted less than a minute.

The madman turned up the light again.

The policeman rose slowly to his feet and stared for a moment at the sheet. Then, with a bound he was at the wall, prodding it with his truncheon. The wall was quite solid. He turned.

'That was Hyde Park,' he said accusingly. 'I recognised it. Where did it come from? And where's it gone to?'

The madman tapped the box triumphantly. 'It's in here,' he said. 'Like a magic lantern.'

'But it moved.'

A seraphic smile lit the madman's face. 'Yes, it moved. It's taken me fifteen years to get to that. But I've done it at last. The picture moves.'

Thus it came about that the first public audience to see a celluloid motion picture film consisted of one London policeman.

The real name of the man who called himself William Friese-Greene was William Edward Green, and he was born in Bristol on September 7, 1855. He was the youngest of seven children, and at the age of fourteen he was apprenticed by his father, a metalworker, to the new and rapidly expanding trade of photography.

Willie Green became an excellent portrait photographer. In those days clamps were used to hold the sitters rigidly still during the long time-exposures necessary. A photographer who could persuade a woman to look her best with an iron clamp sticking in the back of her neck was a novelty in Bristol. Young Mr Green had a way with him. His way, no doubt, would seem a trifle indigestible nowadays (part of it consisted of likening the sitter's hands to the petals of a flower), but in the seventies it was delicious. When he was twenty, Willie Green borrowed enough money to open a studio of his own. In that year, too, he married.

Helena Friese was the daughter of an impoverished Swiss baron, and she had come to England to earn her living as a lady's companion. Ill-health had forced her to give up this work and convalesce with a relative in Bristol. She was dressed in white organdie and reclining decoratively on a black horse-hair sofa when Willie was introduced to her. The most important books on photography were then written in German. She undertook to help him read them.

The wives of inventors have always been long-suffering women. Mental and physical toughness of a very high order seem to have been minimum qualifications for the role. There never could have been a less promising candidate for it than Helena Friese. Not merely had she been 'gently' brought up; she was also a chronic asthmatic and the possessor of what Victorian medicine described as 'a delicate constitution.' In addition, she was 'nervous.' Once, when Willie unexpectedly presented her with a live crab which he had found on the sea-shore, the shock sent her to bed for a week. Happily, if paradoxically, she also had two other qualities; the ability to love and great courage.

She was to need them both.

It is difficult to say precisely when Willie Green became actively concerned with the problem of making pictures move. We know that even at the time of his marriage he was already working on improvements in the chemical aspects of photographic technique. We also know that he was interested in the phenomenon of persistence of vision, upon which the operation of motion pictures depends. This had been noted by Lucretius in his *De Rerum Natura*, written in the first century B.C. During the first half of the nineteenth century toys had been designed which utilised the phenomenon in an elementary way. These toys—the thaumatrope and the zoetrope were among the earliest—had a common pattern. A disc or cylinder was decorated with series drawings of a simple piece of action, such as a dog jumping over a gate, and made to revolve. An illusion of movement was thus created. The dog jumped over the gate and then the action was repeated. The extent of the action was limited by the size of the cylinder or disc.

Willie Green opened his first studio in Bath. He was soon in financial difficulties, and when his daughter Ethel was born he was compelled to pawn his stock of plates to pay the doctor. This was the beginning of an acquaintance with pawnbrokers which was to last throughout his life. However, he had his moments of prosperity. He was a good photographer and the quality of his work gradually became known. Within two or three years there were Friese-Greene Studios (he had added his wife's name to his own and tacked an 'e' on the end) in Bristol and Plymouth as well as in Bath. There he met J. A. R. Rudge.

Rudge was an instrument maker and an inventor of some repute. He was also a friend of Fox Talbot, the man who had invented the photographic process which had superseded Daguerre's. Both men were to have a profound effect upon Willie's future.

Rudge had designed a machine called the bio-phantascope which projected series photographs of movement on a screen. Willie suggested an improvement, a revolving shutter to prevent blurring of the image, and in 1885 the two gave public demonstrations of the machine.

Yet Willie was dissatisfied. The phantascope carried only twelve pictures. Even Muybridge had done better than that! Muybridge was an Englishman who, in 1872, had been able to settle a bet for Leland Stanford in California. Stanford had contended that during a gallop there were moments when a horse had all four feet off the ground. By photographing a horse in motion with twenty-four consecutively operated cameras Muybridge had been able to prove Stanford right. But Willie's idea was that it ought to be possible to take hundreds of such pictures. The problem was how to take them with only one camera. Obviously, the root of the matter was in the nature of the photographic base. Glass was unmanageable. Something else had to be found. Willie at last decided to take Fox Talbot's advice. 'You ought to go to London,' the old man had said. 'London is the place to go if you want to share in the important developments in this remarkable age.'

So the Friese-Greenes abandoned the successful studios in Bath, Bristol and Plymouth, and went to London to open a studio there. After a while, Willie found it necessary to take a partner with money. The name of this unfortunate man was Collings.

To begin with, the firm of Collings and Friese-Greene was highly successful. They opened studios in Bond Street and Piccadilly, and then in Sloane Street. They were 'court photographers.' The titles of two of Willie's entries in the Royal Photographic Society's Exhibition of 1886 are evocative. One was 'Portrait of a Lady in Court Dress'; the other, 'Oh . . . ah!—Portrait of a Child.' But behind the dainty studio in which these confections were produced was a laboratory; and every penny made by Friese-Greene, the court photographer, was promptly appropriated and spent by Willie Green, the inventor.

In 1888 Willie demonstrated before the Bath Photographic Society the first fruits of his work in London, some paper 'films' of street scenes in Brighton. The paper was made transparent by soaking it in oil; but it tore frequently, and he was already at work on a new substance he had found—celluloid. At the time it was available only in thick gluelike sheets. The transparent celluloid film produced by George Eastman in America was yet to come. Willie Green made his own strips of film in the basement of his house; and he designed a new camera for it. By the end of the year his preoccupation with this work and neglect of his ordinary photographic business was complete. Collings at last rebelled, and the partnership was dissolved. Willie Green was on his own again.

The patent for the successful camera which Willie demonstrated to the policeman was taken out in the spring of 1889. It was not the first motion picture to be patented—that of Le Prince, the Frenchman, patented in 1888, has that distinction —but it was the first practical one. It had, indeed, almost all the essential features of a modern camera except sprockets, and these Willie had discarded because, in the earlier paper-film camera, they tore the paper. Willie's patent forestalled by months Edison's demonstration of the kinetoscope and by several years the Lumière brothers' machine.

Two years later Willie was bankrupt.

Before he died, in 1921, he was to go bankrupt twice again; but that first bankruptcy was the greatest disaster, for it cost Helena her life. With extraordinary determination this semi-invalid set about rebuilding her husband's fortunes with the proceeds of the sale of her jewellery. By 1895, Willie again had a photographer's business (owned by Helena) and a laboratory in which he was working on a colour film process. But the strain had been too much for her, and towards the end of that year she died.

He married again eventually, and went on inventing; but he never surpassed his first great achievement. He made money sometimes. More often he lost it. When he died he had over seventy-five patents to his credit; but the all-important patent of 1889 no longer existed. When the first renewal fell due in 1894, he took no action. He did not have five pounds for the renewal fee.

Willie Green was not a man who cared much about his personal dignity or standing in the world. Indeed, the only occasion on which he ever attempted to establish his claim to consideration as a film pioneer was when one of his sons, who had claimed at school that his father had invented the motion-picture camera, was humiliated by the production of an *Encyclopædia Britannica* article on the history of the films which did not even mention his name.

The *Encyclopædia Britannica* has never repaired the omission.

5

The Novelist and the Film-Makers

A great many novels have been written about the experiences
of novelists who have ventured into that strange jungle
called the film industry. Some are funny, many are dull, a
few are angry; but most of them have a common pattern.

The hero, young, innocent, but remarkably talented, has
written a brilliant novel. His agent has persuaded him, though
against his better judgment, to sell the film rights. The producer, generally of Middle-European origin, implores the
hero to write the script. How else can they hope to convey to
the screen the qualities that made the book so successful?
Reluctantly, the hero agrees. Work begins.

Then, disaster strikes. The hero's script is mangled beyond
recognition in order to provide a part for a nymphomaniac
star. The producer turns out to be a pimping monster. The
novel—'this sensitive study of adolescence' as one critic called
it—becomes a roaring musical about campus life in the Middle
West. The novelist returns sadder, wiser, and sick at heart to
the battered old desk in his mother's attic.

That, then, is the legend, and I think that any discussion of
the relationship between the writer and the film industry must
begin by taking it into account. And not merely for the purpose of discrediting it. A great many writers have had encounters with the industry of just that sort. Not all of them,

however, write books to celebrate the occasion. Some, less hampered by self-pity or complacency, have reflected that an art which at its best is capable of making all but the very good novels seem flatulent and commonplace, cannot be judged solely by the activities of its meanest practitioners. I referred to the film industry as a jungle and I hope presently to justify the term. It is not entirely derogatory; jungles are often interesting places. But, if I may pursue the metaphor for the moment, I do not think that a man who goes big game hunting armed only with a catapult is entitled to much sympathy when he gets mauled.

Most writers from other media go to work in the film industry in the hope of making a lot of money in a comparatively short time. That is not intended to be a harsh judgment. It is a good thing to be able to earn a lot of money in a comparatively short time, and only the envious will be ready to supply moral reasons for denying the fact. The nice difference between *making* a lot of money and *earning* it, we will leave for the moment. However, the seduction scene in which the novelist succumbs to the producer's blandishments had better be rewritten, I think; and we ought to add another sequence in which the novelist discusses the tax implications of his surrender with his agent.

Let us look at the producer's point of view. The reasons that he is employing the novelist are fairly complex.

For the business-like folk who control the industry any argument about the merits of a picture can be settled immediately by reference to its takings at the box office. It is idle to complain about this. Film-making is a big business. It must be. For a capital risk of two thousand pounds it is still possible to publish a novel. Five thousand pounds will still finance the production of a play. But even a modest feature involves the investment of hundreds of thousands of pounds.

The position of the producer, then, is a difficult one. The manufacturing process involved in the making of a film is so costly that he cannot take a small risk; he cannot, so to speak, print a thousand copies of something that he feels is promising. He can make a small*ish* picture, but not a very small one; and even with a smallish one he will have to be careful, for the cinema owners are likely to tell him that the public do not want to see smallish pictures, only very big ones, and that they cannot give him any screen time. On the other hand—for, contrary to the general belief, many producers are cultivated and humane men—he knows that the film-going public is not on the whole nearly as stupid as film exhibitors like to insist, and that if he can make a better, more intelligent film than the average, it may be very successful indeed at the box office. And it may not, of course. A film can be acclaimed by the critics and still do no business. A limited, little-theatre, 'prestige' release can be financially disastrous.

The producer, then, is driven to working within a small area of compromise. He can be unusual but not very unusual, intelligent but not very intelligent, honourable but not completely honest. If he chooses an unusual subject he will take care to appease the money people by getting big name stars to play in it, whether they are suitable or not. If his subject requires that sexual relations between human beings be treated at all explicitly, he will accept in advance the film's emasculation by the censors. If he decides to be forthright and controversial, his decision will be flavoured by the knowledge that cinema-goers of every race, religion, and sect (outside the Communist countries, of course) must approve of it, too. Before he begins to share in any profits that may be forthcoming, the picture has to earn very much more than its original negative cost—double as a rule. The domestic market alone is not enough. It is not a simple question of greed either. His status in the industry—and that means the extent of his freedom to do the films he wants—depends not on the aesthetic qualities of his productions, but on how much they gross.

He would not be human if the sum of these pressures did not make him look for some sort of insurance.

There are, of course, several recognised policies available. He can make low-budget horror pictures about mad scientists, with special effects from Mars. He can make pseudo-Biblical pictures. He can even settle for a commercial television series. Usually, however, he adopts a less desperate, though more difficult, course. He competes with other producers for the stars believed to have drawing power at the box office. To get them he needs two things: stories and scripts.

For his story material he looks first to the best-seller lists and the theatrical successes. The reason is that such material, however unsuitable it may be for adaptation to the screen, is 'pre-sold' to the public. That fact will help him not only when it comes to selling the picture, but in engaging the interest of important stars. In the United States this pre-selling is so important that, in the case of a book, it is not uncommon for a producer to subsidise the publisher with special advertising appropriations to maintain sales and keep the book on the best-seller lists.

However, the supply of both best-sellers and theatrical successes is limited, and the motion picture rights to them are costly. Without major studio or other substantial backing, an independent producer is forced to look elsewhere. 'Elsewhere' means, of course, among the less successful books and plays. It is not quite as depressing a task as it may sound. In spite of the relentless year-in-year-out coverage of published work by studio story departments a lot of potential film material remains unsold. Story fashions change, a writer's later success

may stimulate interest in earlier work, censorship require-
ments may be modified so that a story becomes permissible
film material. And while it may not be pre-sold, there is a
compensation: because it has been on the market so long, it
can be bought for a small fraction of the price of a best-seller.

As I want to present both sides of the curious relationship
between writer and producer as faithfully as possible I have
invented a case history. The characters in it are a writer, a
novel, a producer and a film adapted from the novel.

The writer's name is Jerome Anders and I have made him a
novelist rather than a playwright because I know more about
novelists. He is in his late twenties, married with two children,
and works in a bookshop in Kensington. His father was a min-
ing engineer and he spent two years of his early childhood in
Bolivia. He began with short stories and sold three of them.
Henceforth to Seek was his first novel. It had some very good
reviews and sold three thousand copies in hard covers. None
of the cheap edition publishers took it. His second book was
not published. He is working on a third. He would like to
write for his living.

Now for the book. Here is part of the blurb which the publisher's editor wrote for the wrapper of *Henceforth to Seek*:
'This exciting first novel is a lyrical love story based on an old
legend of the Bolivian Indians dealing with the age-long quest
for the ideal woman. Born in London, Anders spent most of
his childhood in Bolivia. The title comes from a poem he
wrote when he was eighteen:

> *Drive me not out; I go unbound*
> *henceforth to seek,*
> *Another love beyond the ice-drenched*
> *slopes of Mana.'*

I will not weary you with the plot.

The producer is in his early fifties. He was originally an actor, became a stage producer and then directed a number of inexpensive films based on successful stage comedies. Later, he produced two very popular war pictures about the R.A.F. One of them was awarded an Oscar for black-and-white photography. He is a Cambridge man.

In recent years his films have been less successful; no real disasters, but no hits either. He is in a mood to experiment with fresh ideas and new people.

As he himself puts it to an interviewing newspaper columnist. 'Nowadays, it seems to me, most producers approach a property they've bought as if it were an enemy that has somehow to be defeated. I say "why buy it if you don't want to use it?" I believe in *Henceforth to Seek* and I'm going to make it the way it is, as frankly and honestly as I know how. Of course, we're going to run into censorship trouble. Very well, I say, let's run into it. If this picture fails in integrity it fails, full stop. That's one of the reasons I've asked the author to write the screenplay.'

It is *one* of the reasons. There are others.

Good screenwriters are expensive. They are also inclined to prefer their own ideas to this particular producer's. He likes writers to be inexpensive and amenable; and if this also means that they are inexperienced, then he is quite ready to repair the deficiency out of his own store of expertise. Or as he prefers to put it: 'As I see it the whole function of the producer is to create enthusiasm and identity of intention within the small creative group which really makes the picture, to give that group a dynamic of its own.'

This is what Anders tells his wife about the producer after their first conference:

'He's not at all what I'd imagined. Looks a bit like a don. Tweeds, bow tie, quiet, relaxed, well-read, articulate. And he's genuinely fond of *Henceforth*. I told him I thought he was insane to try to make a film of it. He said he thought he was insane, too, and why didn't we start Monday? I liked him.'

Three weeks go by. Anders says to his wife:

'Do you know that you can alter the whole emotional content of a scene simply by editing it differently in the cutting room? No, darling, nobody's trying to alter anything. It'll be months before they even start shooting the picture. But the technical side of it's pretty important. I'm glad I've got him on my side. He has an extraordinary grasp of story construction. Makes me feel like an amateur. I'm beginning to realise how little I know about writing for the screen. You know that passage in the book where the young girl about to marry thinks of the lover she has killed? It took me three pages to describe what she was thinking. He wants to do it in one shot of her looking down at a cup of water and then slowly letting the water dribble away into the sand. I wish I'd thought of that. Do you know, I think this might turn out to be a rather better film than it was a novel. Anyway, I'm enjoying myself.'

Three months later the producer says to his wife:

'It's a pity, and I understand how Anders feels; but if we're going to have Cary playing the lover we do have to think again about the story. It's not that I particularly mind his being killed off before the end of the picture—I hope I can rise above that sort of consideration, whatever pressure his agent brings to bear—it's the censorship question. Cary's name should sell the picture, but with the deal he has, and in colour, it's going to cost nearer three times the original budget. I think we have to face the censorship question now. You know I liked the story as it was, but one has to be practical. Besides, I've been wondering anyway, if family audiences are going to like the girl killing one man and then marrying another. I think they'll think it's in bad taste.'

By now the love affair is over. A hack writer has been brought in to do what the producer calls a quick polish on the screenplay.

This is what the hack says:

'Not a playable scene or a speakable line in the entire script. Otherwise it's fine. They start shooting next week. I'd better get to work.'

At the showing of the finished picture, the producer talks to the distributors. They are reasonably happy, but he has something on his mind. Anders is making trouble. For one thing he is demanding that his name be removed from the credit titles. Worse, he got a little tight at a cocktail party and told a disagreeable, but true, and rather funny, story about the producer. A newspaper gossip columnist was there and the story was published. The producer thinks it wise to demonstrate his magnanimity.

'Anders didn't do a bad job on the whole,' he explains; 'but the thing needed reconstructing and a thorough tightening. There were too many characters and not enough action. I got impatient with the girl. The man behaved like an idiot. You see, the trouble with a story of this kind is that it's so easy to be deceived by the writing in the original. Now I could look past all that to the essential story, which was about a man and two girls, with one or two variations and an unusual setting. One of the variations was the killing of the lover, and quite obviously it had to come out in the end. Another thing; the real story didn't begin in the book until chapter eight. With all the dead wood cleared away from the remainder, I was left with very little to work on. I had to invent fresh incident. I'm afraid Anders was a little childish about it. Naturally, he resented things like the introduction of the Cockney sea captain with the lisp; but I felt it needed more comedy. And I was right. A showman has an instinct about these things.'

Three months later the film is out.

'I hear,' says Anders, 'that *Henceforth to Seek* is now called *Beyond the Hills*. You'd think he'd have had the primitive courtesy to send me seats for the premiere, wouldn't you? After all, I wrote it.'

A week after the premiere there is an inquest.

'Of course the snob critics didn't like it,' the producer says defensively; 'but apart from London and Manchester it's doing wonderful business. It's a family picture and that's what this industry needs now . . . good family pictures.'

What about Mr Anders' future?

The money from *Henceforth to Seek* has enabled him to give up his job in the bookshop. He has also leased a cottage in the country and is working there on his new book. Unfortunately, it does not seem to be going very well. The reason, he thinks, is because the country, or that part of it, does not agree with him. Later, when he has moved back to town, he will think of other reasons.

In fact, something has happened to him as a writer during the past few months, and he does not yet know it.

Every writer has a critic inside him and the nature of that critic is very important to his work. It may be benevolent, too benevolent, but it may also be a martinet. If the demands of the internal critic exceed the capacity of the host to pay, or if payment is demanded in an unfamiliar currency, there may be a bankruptcy.

I suggested earlier that, at its best, film-making must be regarded as an art. I make that suggestion again. It is an art. It has therefore a complex discipline. When, then, a comparatively inexperienced writer has a flirtation with it, what he is apt to carry away is not the tender memory of a sweet girl wooed and won, but the faint, patronising smile of a compliant but unsatisfied goddess.

Mr Anders, then, is suffering from a sense of defeat, and the goddess is at his elbow as he works on his new book.

'Do you really think that anyone can play that scene?' she asks.

'I don't care whether anyone can play it or not,' he snaps. 'It's meant to be read.'

'Oops, sorry,' says the goddess; but his working day has been spoiled.

'There are an awful lot of words there,' remarks the goddess a few days later. 'Do you remember that story the producer told you about what you could do with a succession of visual images? It wasn't his own story, of course. It came out of a novel by Scott Fitzgerald. And what was that other anecdote about visual story-telling, the one Schulberg quoted in *What Makes Sammy Run?* Schulberg, now. He's a novelist and a good screenwriter, too.'

Crude? Well yes; but, in spite of what the studio writer did, there was just one scene in *Beyond the Hills* that really worked beautifully; and it was a scene that Anders had imagined and written. At that moment—it lasted two minutes—the screen came to life. When he went out to the studio while they were shooting the picture, it was the only scene the director discussed with him. He has had a tantalising glimpse of just how satisfying the medium can be.

It has been said that the problem of screen-writing is to say much in little, and then take half of that little out, and still preserve an effect of leisure and natural movement. It has also been said, again and again, that the film is still primarily a visual medium. For those unfamiliar with the anecdote of Budd Schulberg's to which I referred, I have summarised it. It illustrates both contentions.

A playwright employed to work on the script of a film writes a scene lasting five minutes, to explain that a man is tired of his wife and that she knows it. The scene is wittily written and would be superb on the stage. But on the screen the time convention is different. Five minutes can seem like an eternity. So the producer asks an old silent film director how he would write such a scene at the opening of a picture. This is what the director tells him:

The husband and wife walk together into a lift. The doors close, the lift starts up. The husband has his hat on. At the next floor the lift stops and an attractive girl gets in. The husband politely takes his hat off. The wife sees him do so and wonders why. Then, she looks at the attractive girl and understands.

No word has been spoken. The total time to make the statement is about thirty seconds.

But to return to the plight of our writer. His fundamental mistake was to suppose that when he was asked to write a screenplay he was being asked to use the same talent that had led him to write the original novel. In fact, screen-writing has very little to do with writing as a novelist understands the term. The only common denominators are a sense of story construction—and in this respect the novel is closer to the film than the play—and the ability to create characters who breathe. It was for those things, not his skill as a novelist, that our man was employed; and the knowledge that it was his own novel that he was being asked to adapt only helped to obscure the fact.

Why should that ignorance be so disastrous?

I have said that the novelist has a critic inside him. It is a very necessary part of his equipment, because if he is any sort of a story-teller he also has a considerable sense of omnipotence. In his private world he is an absolute ruler with godlike powers of control over his creatures. This control—call it inner confidence, sureness of touch, anything you will—is vitally important to him. It is at the core of his ability to work as a writer. What happens when he encounters the film-makers is that, for the first time, that absolute control is challenged. It must be. Between the novelist and his readers the line of communication is almost direct, via his publisher. But between the screenwriter and his audience there stands not only an intricate manufacturing process, but also a producer, a director, an art director, a number of actors, a lighting cameraman, a film editor, and a sound engineer. Many of them are intelligent, talented, and amiable persons. The trouble is that, in their various fields, they are likely to be as omnipotently disposed as the writer, and, indeed, will not be very much good at their jobs if they are not. In the resultant hurly-burly of conflicting egos and interests, even actors sometimes have difficulty in preserving their self-esteem. The novelist, used to the enemies within, but utterly confounded when he finds them outside, generally goes down like a ninepin.

There are several ways in which the novelist attempts to deal with the challenge.

He may refuse it altogether and retire, suffused with indignation, to write one of those novels about his experiences which I began by mentioning. That way, he may in due course repair the damage he has suffered. Whether or not he wholly succeeds depends on how good the book is.

Or he may decide to fight for his work as a screenwriter and attempt to protect it from the film-making machinery; as he would try to protect his work as a novelist if, for example, a publisher's editor were to propose changes with which he did not agree. In the case of films, however, he will always lose. No matter how energetic he is and how adept he may be at undermining the confidence of his opponents, he can only deal with them separately and they will combine against him. In the film industry the writer is a disagreeable necessity, tolerated by the technicians only because they cannot exercise

their skills until he has done his work. 'Thank God that's over,'
I have heard a producer say when the writer delivered his
script. 'Now we can get down to film-making.' The other
difficulty about this sort of contest is that, unless the writer is
vastly experienced or suffers from delusions of grandeur, he
will find that he is frequently quite wrong in his judgments,
and that the scene that he regarded as indispensable has
turned out, as his opponents predicted it would, a dreadful
bore.

Of course, quite a number of successful screenwriters have
attempted to gain control of the situation by becoming producers or directors. The industry's method of explaining this
change of status is to say that the man in question was 'too
good to be only a writer.' But most of the writer-directors end
by employing other writers to work with them on the scripts,
and I do not know of any professional novelist who has
successfully made that particular transition.

There are, of course, the novelists who, perceiving the challenge, discreetly decide to ignore it. Their plan is to make a
killing and then live richly on the proceeds while they work on
a new book. The picture that is going to be made does not concern them. If the producer wants to bring in another writer to
work on it, by all means let him do so. He, the novelist, wrote
a script; his commitment is ended.

What I envy about these happy men and women is their
hardihood; and I am unsympathetic when they complain, as
they do, that they never have much success where films are
concerned. I think that they have a great deal of success;
though not often twice with the same producer.

However, most novelists who become embroiled in this
maddening business are not so sturdy. The film-industry, in
fact, has become a kind of occupational hazard for writers. It
is not much use just advising them to avoid it. One might just

as well advise a matador to refuse to fight bulls of a certain breed. All we can hope is that, when the time comes, no permanent harm will be done, and that, even if the man cannot win, the injury he sustains will not be too painful.

What, then, are the prospects for Mr Anders, struggling wretchedly with a new novel that he no longer believes in, and feelings of incompetence and sterility that are beginning to overwhelm him?

A fifty-fifty chance, I would say. What he will probably do after a while is to abandon the novel he is working on, and turn it into an original story for the screen. If he sells it to a producer, he will probably be asked to work on the script and will agree. This time, he will tell himself, it is going to be different. And it may well be—a little different. He will both argue and write a little more persuasively this time. Sooner or later, he will probably know enough about the curious shorthand of the screen to produce a completely integrated and photographable screenplay. And that will be the moment of decision for him. It is not everyone who can fertilise the sacred cow, and he may find the experience deeply satisfying. If he does, then, as a novelist, his goose is cooked. But if, and this is possible, all that he experiences is a sense of anti-climax, a feeling of irritation because his work must now be handed over to others, yet not sufficient irritation to make him want to do the rest of the work himself, there is hope. It will not be long before he is back working in a medium in which he can be fully creative; in which he can forget for a while the sacred cow and its attendant male nurses, and function again not only as a father to the child, but as mother, doctor, and midwife also.

Is this, then, after all, a simple dilemma—fulfilment or frustration? Fulfilled he stays, frustrated he leaves? I think that for some writers it proves to be so. For others, however, the issue is not so clear-cut.

A distinguished producer complained recently that writers in other media—novelists and playwrights in particular—are hostile to the industry. He went on to warn them that the writer who goes into films has to accept the fact that he is no longer his own boss, and to learn to like it.

I have worked with that producer happily on two pictures. He is very far from being a bossy man himself. Perhaps that is why writers like working with him. No one, then, should know better then he that the writer who is not his own creative master is no longer a writer worth employing; he has become a hack. To be one's own master in this sense is not to be a megalomaniac, impervious to reason and incapable of compromise. The problem of the writer in the industry, indeed, is the problem of the director, the actor, the producer, and everyone else concerned creatively with production. It is the problem of collaboration without loss of self-respect. The effort to solve that problem is, in essence, the effort to attain maturity. However painful it may be, that seems to me an effort always worth making; and not only in the film industry.